C-1142 CAREER EXAMINATION SERIES

This is your
PASSBOOK for...

Bridge Operations Supervisor

Test Preparation Study Guide
Questions & Answers

COPYRIGHT NOTICE

This book is SOLELY intended for, is sold ONLY to, and its use is RESTRICTED to individual, bona fide applicants or candidates who qualify by virtue of having seriously filed applications for appropriate license, certificate, professional and/or promotional advancement, higher school matriculation, scholarship, or other legitimate requirements of education and/or governmental authorities.

This book is NOT intended for use, class instruction, tutoring, training, duplication, copying, reprinting, excerption, or adaptation, etc., by:

1) Other publishers
2) Proprietors and/or Instructors of "Coaching" and/or Preparatory Courses
3) Personnel and/or Training Divisions of commercial, industrial, and governmental organizations
4) Schools, colleges, or universities and/or their departments and staffs, including teachers and other personnel
5) Testing Agencies or Bureaus
6) Study groups which seek by the purchase of a single volume to copy and/or duplicate and/or adapt this material for use by the group as a whole without having purchased individual volumes for each of the members of the group
7) Et al.

Such persons would be in violation of appropriate Federal and State statutes.

PROVISION OF LICENSING AGREEMENTS – Recognized educational, commercial, industrial, and governmental institutions and organizations, and others legitimately engaged in educational pursuits, including training, testing, and measurement activities, may address request for a licensing agreement to the copyright owners, who will determine whether, and under what conditions, including fees and charges, the materials in this book may be used them. In other words, a licensing facility exists for the legitimate use of the material in this book on other than an individual basis. However, it is asseverated and affirmed here that the material in this book CANNOT be used without the receipt of the express permission of such a licensing agreement from the Publishers. Inquiries re licensing should be addressed to the company, attention rights and permissions department.

All rights reserved, including the right of reproduction in whole or in part, in any form or by any means, electronic or mechanical, including photocopying, recording, or by any information storage and retrieval system, without permission in writing from the Publisher.

Copyright © 2025 by
National Learning Corporation

212 Michael Drive, Syosset, NY 11791
(516) 921-8888 • www.passbooks.com
E-mail: info@passbooks.com

PASSBOOK® SERIES

THE *PASSBOOK® SERIES* has been created to prepare applicants and candidates for the ultimate academic battlefield – the examination room.

At some time in our lives, each and every one of us may be required to take an examination – for validation, matriculation, admission, qualification, registration, certification, or licensure.

Based on the assumption that every applicant or candidate has met the basic formal educational standards, has taken the required number of courses, and read the necessary texts, the *PASSBOOK® SERIES* furnishes the one special preparation which may assure passing with confidence, instead of failing with insecurity. Examination questions – together with answers – are furnished as the basic vehicle for study so that the mysteries of the examination and its compounding difficulties may be eliminated or diminished by a sure method.

This book is meant to help you pass your examination provided that you qualify and are serious in your objective.

The entire field is reviewed through the huge store of content information which is succinctly presented through a provocative and challenging approach – the question-and-answer method.

A climate of success is established by furnishing the correct answers at the end of each test.

You soon learn to recognize types of questions, forms of questions, and patterns of questioning. You may even begin to anticipate expected outcomes.

You perceive that many questions are repeated or adapted so that you can gain acute insights, which may enable you to score many sure points.

You learn how to confront new questions, or types of questions, and to attack them confidently and work out the correct answers.

You note objectives and emphases, and recognize pitfalls and dangers, so that you may make positive educational adjustments.

Moreover, you are kept fully informed in relation to new concepts, methods, practices, and directions in the field.

You discover that you are actually taking the examination all the time: you are preparing for the examination by "taking" an examination, not by reading extraneous and/or supererogatory textbooks.

In short, this PASSBOOK®, used directedly, should be an important factor in helping you to pass your test.

BRIDGE OPERATIONS SUPERVISOR

DUTIES:
Performs technical and supervisory work directing the safe operation and maintenance of bridges; performs related duties as required.

EXAMPLES OF TYPICAL TASKS:
Supervises and directs the activities of assistant bridge operators, bridge operators and other personnel assigned to the operation, care and maintenance of bridges. Establishes procedures, schedules, assignments and enforces the rules and regulations of the department and governmental agencies. Inspects electrical, mechanical and manual operating equipment and bridge structures to ensure efficiency and safety. Investigates and reports on accidents and complaints involving all bridge operating personnel. Controls the issuance of supplies, materials and equipment; maintains inventory and requisitions supplies as needed. Prepares and supervises the preparation of reports on vehicular and marine traffic counts, quarterly and annual openings, employee attendance and payroll. Receives and acts on reports submitted by bridge operators-in-charge. Collaborates with the department of sanitation on snow removal from bridges and other approaches. Drives a motor vehicle as required in the performance of his duties.

SUBJECT OF EXAMINATION:
The written test is designed to test for knowledge, skills, and/or abilities in such areas as:
1. **Bridge operation and the repair of mechanical and electrical equipment on bridges** - These questions test for knowledge of the principles and practices involved in the operation, maintenance and repair of the mechanical and electrical equipment typically found on various types of bridges.
2. **Bridge reconstruction, maintenance and repair** - These questions test for knowledge of the proper methods, materials, and equipment used in the upkeep of bridges and bridge abutments and may include such areas as concrete and pavement maintenance, steel maintenance including sandblasting, painting, and welding, appropriate environmental and worker protection safeguards, and snow and ice removal and control.
3. **Safety practices** - These questions test for knowledge of and the ability to apply safety principles related to construction and maintenance work zones, including traffic control, the safe use of equipment, and the overall safety of workers, the traveling public, and the work environment.
4. **Supervision** - These questions test for knowledge of the principles and practices employed in planning, organizing, and controlling the activities of a work unit toward predetermined objectives. The concepts covered, usually in a situational question format, include such topics as assigning and reviewing work; evaluating performance; maintaining work standards; motivating and developing subordinates; implementing procedural change; increasing efficiency; and dealing with problems of absenteeism, morale, and discipline.

HOW TO TAKE A TEST

I. YOU MUST PASS AN EXAMINATION

A. WHAT EVERY CANDIDATE SHOULD KNOW

Examination applicants often ask us for help in preparing for the written test. What can I study in advance? What kinds of questions will be asked? How will the test be given? How will the papers be graded?

As an applicant for a civil service examination, you may be wondering about some of these things. Our purpose here is to suggest effective methods of advance study and to describe civil service examinations.

Your chances for success on this examination can be increased if you know how to prepare. Those "pre-examination jitters" can be reduced if you know what to expect. You can even experience an adventure in good citizenship if you know why civil service exams are given.

B. WHY ARE CIVIL SERVICE EXAMINATIONS GIVEN?

Civil service examinations are important to you in two ways. As a citizen, you want public jobs filled by employees who know how to do their work. As a job seeker, you want a fair chance to compete for that job on an equal footing with other candidates. The best-known means of accomplishing this two-fold goal is the competitive examination.

Exams are widely publicized throughout the nation. They may be administered for jobs in federal, state, city, municipal, town or village governments or agencies.

Any citizen may apply, with some limitations, such as the age or residence of applicants. Your experience and education may be reviewed to see whether you meet the requirements for the particular examination. When these requirements exist, they are reasonable and applied consistently to all applicants. Thus, a competitive examination may cause you some uneasiness now, but it is your privilege and safeguard.

C. HOW ARE CIVIL SERVICE EXAMS DEVELOPED?

Examinations are carefully written by trained technicians who are specialists in the field known as "psychological measurement," in consultation with recognized authorities in the field of work that the test will cover. These experts recommend the subject matter areas or skills to be tested; only those knowledges or skills important to your success on the job are included. The most reliable books and source materials available are used as references. Together, the experts and technicians judge the difficulty level of the questions.

Test technicians know how to phrase questions so that the problem is clearly stated. Their ethics do not permit "trick" or "catch" questions. Questions may have been tried out on sample groups, or subjected to statistical analysis, to determine their usefulness.

Written tests are often used in combination with performance tests, ratings of training and experience, and oral interviews. All of these measures combine to form the best-known means of finding the right person for the right job.

II. HOW TO PASS THE WRITTEN TEST

A. NATURE OF THE EXAMINATION

To prepare intelligently for civil service examinations, you should know how they differ from school examinations you have taken. In school you were assigned certain definite pages to read or subjects to cover. The examination questions were quite detailed and usually emphasized memory. Civil service exams, on the other hand, try to discover your present ability to perform the duties of a position, plus your potentiality to learn these duties. In other words, a civil service exam attempts to predict how successful you will be. Questions cover such a broad area that they cannot be as minute and detailed as school exam questions.

In the public service similar kinds of work, or positions, are grouped together in one "class." This process is known as *position-classification*. All the positions in a class are paid according to the salary range for that class. One class title covers all of these positions, and they are all tested by the same examination.

B. FOUR BASIC STEPS

1) Study the announcement

How, then, can you know what subjects to study? Our best answer is: "Learn as much as possible about the class of positions for which you've applied." The exam will test the knowledge, skills and abilities needed to do the work.

Your most valuable source of information about the position you want is the official exam announcement. This announcement lists the training and experience qualifications. Check these standards and apply only if you come reasonably close to meeting them.

The brief description of the position in the examination announcement offers some clues to the subjects which will be tested. Think about the job itself. Review the duties in your mind. Can you perform them, or are there some in which you are rusty? Fill in the blank spots in your preparation.

Many jurisdictions preview the written test in the exam announcement by including a section called "Knowledge and Abilities Required," "Scope of the Examination," or some similar heading. Here you will find out specifically what fields will be tested.

2) Review your own background

Once you learn in general what the position is all about, and what you need to know to do the work, ask yourself which subjects you already know fairly well and which need improvement. You may wonder whether to concentrate on improving your strong areas or on building some background in your fields of weakness. When the announcement has specified "some knowledge" or "considerable knowledge," or has used adjectives like "beginning principles of..." or "advanced ... methods," you can get a clue as to the number and difficulty of questions to be asked in any given field. More questions, and hence broader coverage, would be included for those subjects which are more important in the work. Now weigh your strengths and weaknesses against the job requirements and prepare accordingly.

3) Determine the level of the position

Another way to tell how intensively you should prepare is to understand the level of the job for which you are applying. Is it the entering level? In other words, is this the position in which beginners in a field of work are hired? Or is it an intermediate or advanced level? Sometimes this is indicated by such words as "Junior" or "Senior" in the class title. Other jurisdictions use Roman numerals to designate the level – Clerk I, Clerk II, for example. The word "Supervisor" sometimes appears in the title. If the level is not indicated by the title, check the description of duties. Will you be working under very close supervision, or will you have responsibility for independent decisions in this work?

4) Choose appropriate study materials

Now that you know the subjects to be examined and the relative amount of each subject to be covered, you can choose suitable study materials. For beginning level jobs, or even advanced ones, if you have a pronounced weakness in some aspect of your training, read a modern, standard textbook in that field. Be sure it is up to date and has general coverage. Such books are normally available at your library, and the librarian will be glad to help you locate one. For entry-level positions, questions of appropriate difficulty are chosen – neither highly advanced questions, nor those too simple. Such questions require careful thought but not advanced training.

If the position for which you are applying is technical or advanced, you will read more advanced, specialized material. If you are already familiar with the basic principles of your field, elementary textbooks would waste your time. Concentrate on advanced textbooks and technical periodicals. Think through the concepts and review difficult problems in your field.

These are all general sources. You can get more ideas on your own initiative, following these leads. For example, training manuals and publications of the government agency which employs workers in your field can be useful, particularly for technical and professional positions. A letter or visit to the government department involved may result in more specific study suggestions, and certainly will provide you with a more definite idea of the exact nature of the position you are seeking.

III. KINDS OF TESTS

Tests are used for purposes other than measuring knowledge and ability to perform specified duties. For some positions, it is equally important to test ability to make adjustments to new situations or to profit from training. In others, basic mental abilities not dependent on information are essential. Questions which test these things may not appear as pertinent to the duties of the position as those which test for knowledge and information. Yet they are often highly important parts of a fair examination. For very general questions, it is almost impossible to help you direct your study efforts. What we can do is to point out some of the more common of these general abilities needed in public service positions and describe some typical questions.

1) General information

Broad, general information has been found useful for predicting job success in some kinds of work. This is tested in a variety of ways, from vocabulary lists to questions about current events. Basic background in some field of work, such as sociology or economics, may be sampled in a group of questions. Often these are principles which have become familiar to most persons through exposure rather than through formal training. It is difficult to advise you how to study for these questions; being alert to the world around you is our best suggestion.

2) Verbal ability

An example of an ability needed in many positions is verbal or language ability. Verbal ability is, in brief, the ability to use and understand words. Vocabulary and grammar tests are typical measures of this ability. Reading comprehension or paragraph interpretation questions are common in many kinds of civil service tests. You are given a paragraph of written material and asked to find its central meaning.

3) Numerical ability

Number skills can be tested by the familiar arithmetic problem, by checking paired lists of numbers to see which are alike and which are different, or by interpreting charts and graphs. In the latter test, a graph may be printed in the test booklet which you are asked to use as the basis for answering questions.

4) Observation

A popular test for law-enforcement positions is the observation test. A picture is shown to you for several minutes, then taken away. Questions about the picture test your ability to observe both details and larger elements.

5) Following directions

In many positions in the public service, the employee must be able to carry out written instructions dependably and accurately. You may be given a chart with several columns, each column listing a variety of information. The questions require you to carry out directions involving the information given in the chart.

6) Skills and aptitudes

Performance tests effectively measure some manual skills and aptitudes. When the skill is one in which you are trained, such as typing or shorthand, you can practice. These tests are often very much like those given in business school or high school courses. For many of the other skills and aptitudes, however, no short-time preparation can be made. Skills and abilities natural to you or that you have developed throughout your lifetime are being tested.

Many of the general questions just described provide all the data needed to answer the questions and ask you to use your reasoning ability to find the answers. Your best preparation for these tests, as well as for tests of facts and ideas, is to be at your physical and mental best. You, no doubt, have your own methods of getting into an exam-taking mood and keeping "in shape." The next section lists some ideas on this subject.

IV. KINDS OF QUESTIONS

Only rarely is the "essay" question, which you answer in narrative form, used in civil service tests. Civil service tests are usually of the short-answer type. Full instructions for answering these questions will be given to you at the examination. But in case this is your first experience with short-answer questions and separate answer sheets, here is what you need to know:

1) Multiple-choice Questions

Most popular of the short-answer questions is the "multiple choice" or "best answer" question. It can be used, for example, to test for factual knowledge, ability to solve problems or judgment in meeting situations found at work.

A multiple-choice question is normally one of three types—
- It can begin with an incomplete statement followed by several possible endings. You are to find the one ending which *best* completes the statement, although some of the others may not be entirely wrong.
- It can also be a complete statement in the form of a question which is answered by choosing one of the statements listed.

- It can be in the form of a problem – again you select the best answer.

Here is an example of a multiple-choice question with a discussion which should give you some clues as to the method for choosing the right answer:

When an employee has a complaint about his assignment, the action which will *best* help him overcome his difficulty is to
- A. discuss his difficulty with his coworkers
- B. take the problem to the head of the organization
- C. take the problem to the person who gave him the assignment
- D. say nothing to anyone about his complaint

In answering this question, you should study each of the choices to find which is best. Consider choice "A" – Certainly an employee may discuss his complaint with fellow employees, but no change or improvement can result, and the complaint remains unresolved. Choice "B" is a poor choice since the head of the organization probably does not know what assignment you have been given, and taking your problem to him is known as "going over the head" of the supervisor. The supervisor, or person who made the assignment, is the person who can clarify it or correct any injustice. Choice "C" is, therefore, correct. To say nothing, as in choice "D," is unwise. Supervisors have and interest in knowing the problems employees are facing, and the employee is seeking a solution to his problem.

2) True/False Questions

The "true/false" or "right/wrong" form of question is sometimes used. Here a complete statement is given. Your job is to decide whether the statement is right or wrong.

SAMPLE: A roaming cell-phone call to a nearby city costs less than a non-roaming call to a distant city.

This statement is wrong, or false, since roaming calls are more expensive.

This is not a complete list of all possible question forms, although most of the others are variations of these common types. You will always get complete directions for answering questions. Be sure you understand *how* to mark your answers – ask questions until you do.

V. RECORDING YOUR ANSWERS

Computer terminals are used more and more today for many different kinds of exams.

For an examination with very few applicants, you may be told to record your answers in the test booklet itself. Separate answer sheets are much more common. If this separate answer sheet is to be scored by machine – and this is often the case – it is highly important that you mark your answers correctly in order to get credit.

An electronic scoring machine is often used in civil service offices because of the speed with which papers can be scored. Machine-scored answer sheets must be marked with a pencil, which will be given to you. This pencil has a high graphite content which responds to the electronic scoring machine. As a matter of fact, stray dots may register as answers, so do not let your pencil rest on the answer sheet while you are pondering the correct answer. Also, if your pencil lead breaks or is otherwise defective, ask for another.

Since the answer sheet will be dropped in a slot in the scoring machine, be careful not to bend the corners or get the paper crumpled.

The answer sheet normally has five vertical columns of numbers, with 30 numbers to a column. These numbers correspond to the question numbers in your test booklet. After each number, going across the page are four or five pairs of dotted lines. These short dotted lines have small letters or numbers above them. The first two pairs may also have a "T" or "F" above the letters. This indicates that the first two pairs only are to be used if the questions are of the true-false type. If the questions are multiple choice, disregard the "T" and "F" and pay attention only to the small letters or numbers.

Answer your questions in the manner of the sample that follows:

32. The largest city in the United States is
    A. Washington, D.C.
    B. New York City
    C. Chicago
    D. Detroit
    E. San Francisco

1) Choose the answer you think is best. (New York City is the largest, so "B" is correct.)
2) Find the row of dotted lines numbered the same as the question you are answering. (Find row number 32)
3) Find the pair of dotted lines corresponding to the answer. (Find the pair of lines under the mark "B.")
4) Make a solid black mark between the dotted lines.

VI. BEFORE THE TEST

Common sense will help you find procedures to follow to get ready for an examination. Too many of us, however, overlook these sensible measures. Indeed, nervousness and fatigue have been found to be the most serious reasons why applicants fail to do their best on civil service tests. Here is a list of reminders:

- Begin your preparation early – Don't wait until the last minute to go scurrying around for books and materials or to find out what the position is all about.
- Prepare continuously – An hour a night for a week is better than an all-night cram session. This has been definitely established. What is more, a night a week for a month will return better dividends than crowding your study into a shorter period of time.
- Locate the place of the exam – You have been sent a notice telling you when and where to report for the examination. If the location is in a different town or otherwise unfamiliar to you, it would be well to inquire the best route and learn something about the building.
- Relax the night before the test – Allow your mind to rest. Do not study at all that night. Plan some mild recreation or diversion; then go to bed early and get a good night's sleep.
- Get up early enough to make a leisurely trip to the place for the test – This way unforeseen events, traffic snarls, unfamiliar buildings, etc. will not upset you.
- Dress comfortably – A written test is not a fashion show. You will be known by number and not by name, so wear something comfortable.

- Leave excess paraphernalia at home – Shopping bags and odd bundles will get in your way. You need bring only the items mentioned in the official notice you received; usually everything you need is provided. Do not bring reference books to the exam. They will only confuse those last minutes and be taken away from you when in the test room.
- Arrive somewhat ahead of time – If because of transportation schedules you must get there very early, bring a newspaper or magazine to take your mind off yourself while waiting.
- Locate the examination room – When you have found the proper room, you will be directed to the seat or part of the room where you will sit. Sometimes you are given a sheet of instructions to read while you are waiting. Do not fill out any forms until you are told to do so; just read them and be prepared.
- Relax and prepare to listen to the instructions
- If you have any physical problem that may keep you from doing your best, be sure to tell the test administrator. If you are sick or in poor health, you really cannot do your best on the exam. You can come back and take the test some other time.

VII. AT THE TEST

The day of the test is here and you have the test booklet in your hand. The temptation to get going is very strong. Caution! There is more to success than knowing the right answers. You must know how to identify your papers and understand variations in the type of short-answer question used in this particular examination. Follow these suggestions for maximum results from your efforts:

1) Cooperate with the monitor

The test administrator has a duty to create a situation in which you can be as much at ease as possible. He will give instructions, tell you when to begin, check to see that you are marking your answer sheet correctly, and so on. He is not there to guard you, although he will see that your competitors do not take unfair advantage. He wants to help you do your best.

2) Listen to all instructions

Don't jump the gun! Wait until you understand all directions. In most civil service tests you get more time than you need to answer the questions. So don't be in a hurry. Read each word of instructions until you clearly understand the meaning. Study the examples, listen to all announcements and follow directions. Ask questions if you do not understand what to do.

3) Identify your papers

Civil service exams are usually identified by number only. You will be assigned a number; you must not put your name on your test papers. Be sure to copy your number correctly. Since more than one exam may be given, copy your exact examination title.

4) Plan your time

Unless you are told that a test is a "speed" or "rate of work" test, speed itself is usually not important. Time enough to answer all the questions will be provided, but this does not mean that you have all day. An overall time limit has been set. Divide the total time (in minutes) by the number of questions to determine the approximate time you have for each question.

5) Do not linger over difficult questions

If you come across a difficult question, mark it with a paper clip (useful to have along) and come back to it when you have been through the booklet. One caution if you do this – be sure to skip a number on your answer sheet as well. Check often to be sure that you have not lost your place and that you are marking in the row numbered the same as the question you are answering.

6) Read the questions

Be sure you know what the question asks! Many capable people are unsuccessful because they failed to *read* the questions correctly.

7) Answer all questions

Unless you have been instructed that a penalty will be deducted for incorrect answers, it is better to guess than to omit a question.

8) Speed tests

It is often better NOT to guess on speed tests. It has been found that on timed tests people are tempted to spend the last few seconds before time is called in marking answers at random – without even reading them – in the hope of picking up a few extra points. To discourage this practice, the instructions may warn you that your score will be "corrected" for guessing. That is, a penalty will be applied. The incorrect answers will be deducted from the correct ones, or some other penalty formula will be used.

9) Review your answers

If you finish before time is called, go back to the questions you guessed or omitted to give them further thought. Review other answers if you have time.

10) Return your test materials

If you are ready to leave before others have finished or time is called, take ALL your materials to the monitor and leave quietly. Never take any test material with you. The monitor can discover whose papers are not complete, and taking a test booklet may be grounds for disqualification.

VIII. EXAMINATION TECHNIQUES

1) Read the general instructions carefully. These are usually printed on the first page of the exam booklet. As a rule, these instructions refer to the timing of the examination; the fact that you should not start work until the signal and must stop work at a signal, etc. If there are any *special* instructions, such as a choice of questions to be answered, make sure that you note this instruction carefully.

2) When you are ready to start work on the examination, that is as soon as the signal has been given, read the instructions to each question booklet, underline any key words or phrases, such as *least, best, outline, describe* and the like. In this way you will tend to answer as requested rather than discover on reviewing your paper that you *listed without describing*, that you selected the *worst* choice rather than the *best* choice, etc.

3) If the examination is of the objective or multiple-choice type – that is, each question will also give a series of possible answers: A, B, C or D, and you are called upon to select the best answer and write the letter next to that answer on your answer paper – it is advisable to start answering each question in turn. There may be anywhere from 50 to 100 such questions in the three or four hours allotted and you can see how much time would be taken if you read through all the questions before beginning to answer any. Furthermore, if you come across a question or group of questions which you know would be difficult to answer, it would undoubtedly affect your handling of all the other questions.

4) If the examination is of the essay type and contains but a few questions, it is a moot point as to whether you should read all the questions before starting to answer any one. Of course, if you are given a choice – say five out of seven and the like – then it is essential to read all the questions so you can eliminate the two that are most difficult. If, however, you are asked to answer all the questions, there may be danger in trying to answer the easiest one first because you may find that you will spend too much time on it. The best technique is to answer the first question, then proceed to the second, etc.

5) Time your answers. Before the exam begins, write down the time it started, then add the time allowed for the examination and write down the time it must be completed, then divide the time available somewhat as follows:
   - If 3-1/2 hours are allowed, that would be 210 minutes. If you have 80 objective-type questions, that would be an average of 2-1/2 minutes per question. Allow yourself no more than 2 minutes per question, or a total of 160 minutes, which will permit about 50 minutes to review.
   - If for the time allotment of 210 minutes there are 7 essay questions to answer, that would average about 30 minutes a question. Give yourself only 25 minutes per question so that you have about 35 minutes to review.

6) The most important instruction is to *read each question* and make sure you know what is wanted. The second most important instruction is to *time yourself properly* so that you answer every question. The third most important instruction is to *answer every question*. Guess if you have to but include something for each question. Remember that you will receive no credit for a blank and will probably receive some credit if you write something in answer to an essay question. If you guess a letter – say "B" for a multiple-choice question – you may have guessed right. If you leave a blank as an answer to a multiple-choice question, the examiners may respect your feelings but it will not add a point to your score. Some exams may penalize you for wrong answers, so in such cases *only*, you may not want to guess unless you have some basis for your answer.

7) Suggestions
   a. Objective-type questions
      1. Examine the question booklet for proper sequence of pages and questions
      2. Read all instructions carefully
      3. Skip any question which seems too difficult; return to it after all other questions have been answered
      4. Apportion your time properly; do not spend too much time on any single question or group of questions

5. Note and underline key words – *all, most, fewest, least, best, worst, same, opposite,* etc.
6. Pay particular attention to negatives
7. Note unusual option, e.g., unduly long, short, complex, different or similar in content to the body of the question
8. Observe the use of "hedging" words – *probably, may, most likely,* etc.
9. Make sure that your answer is put next to the same number as the question
10. Do not second-guess unless you have good reason to believe the second answer is definitely more correct
11. Cross out original answer if you decide another answer is more accurate; do not erase until you are ready to hand your paper in
12. Answer all questions; guess unless instructed otherwise
13. Leave time for review

   b. Essay questions
     1. Read each question carefully
     2. Determine exactly what is wanted. Underline key words or phrases.
     3. Decide on outline or paragraph answer
     4. Include many different points and elements unless asked to develop any one or two points or elements
     5. Show impartiality by giving pros and cons unless directed to select one side only
     6. Make and write down any assumptions you find necessary to answer the questions
     7. Watch your English, grammar, punctuation and choice of words
     8. Time your answers; don't crowd material

8) Answering the essay question

Most essay questions can be answered by framing the specific response around several key words or ideas. Here are a few such key words or ideas:

M's: manpower, materials, methods, money, management
P's: purpose, program, policy, plan, procedure, practice, problems, pitfalls, personnel, public relations

   a. Six basic steps in handling problems:
     1. Preliminary plan and background development
     2. Collect information, data and facts
     3. Analyze and interpret information, data and facts
     4. Analyze and develop solutions as well as make recommendations
     5. Prepare report and sell recommendations
     6. Install recommendations and follow up effectiveness

   b. Pitfalls to avoid
     1. *Taking things for granted* – A statement of the situation does not necessarily imply that each of the elements is necessarily true; for example, a complaint may be invalid and biased so that all that can be taken for granted is that a complaint has been registered

2. *Considering only one side of a situation* – Wherever possible, indicate several alternatives and then point out the reasons you selected the best one
3. *Failing to indicate follow up* – Whenever your answer indicates action on your part, make certain that you will take proper follow-up action to see how successful your recommendations, procedures or actions turn out to be
4. *Taking too long in answering any single question* – Remember to time your answers properly

IX. AFTER THE TEST

Scoring procedures differ in detail among civil service jurisdictions although the general principles are the same. Whether the papers are hand-scored or graded by machine we have described, they are nearly always graded by number. That is, the person who marks the paper knows only the number – never the name – of the applicant. Not until all the papers have been graded will they be matched with names. If other tests, such as training and experience or oral interview ratings have been given, scores will be combined. Different parts of the examination usually have different weights. For example, the written test might count 60 percent of the final grade, and a rating of training and experience 40 percent. In many jurisdictions, veterans will have a certain number of points added to their grades.

After the final grade has been determined, the names are placed in grade order and an eligible list is established. There are various methods for resolving ties between those who get the same final grade – probably the most common is to place first the name of the person whose application was received first. Job offers are made from the eligible list in the order the names appear on it. You will be notified of your grade and your rank as soon as all these computations have been made. This will be done as rapidly as possible.

People who are found to meet the requirements in the announcement are called "eligibles." Their names are put on a list of eligible candidates. An eligible's chances of getting a job depend on how high he stands on this list and how fast agencies are filling jobs from the list.

When a job is to be filled from a list of eligibles, the agency asks for the names of people on the list of eligibles for that job. When the civil service commission receives this request, it sends to the agency the names of the three people highest on this list. Or, if the job to be filled has specialized requirements, the office sends the agency the names of the top three persons who meet these requirements from the general list.

The appointing officer makes a choice from among the three people whose names were sent to him. If the selected person accepts the appointment, the names of the others are put back on the list to be considered for future openings.

That is the rule in hiring from all kinds of eligible lists, whether they are for typist, carpenter, chemist, or something else. For every vacancy, the appointing officer has his choice of any one of the top three eligibles on the list. This explains why the person whose name is on top of the list sometimes does not get an appointment when some of the persons lower on the list do. If the appointing officer chooses the second or third eligible, the No. 1 eligible does not get a job at once, but stays on the list until he is appointed or the list is terminated.

X. HOW TO PASS THE INTERVIEW TEST

The examination for which you applied requires an oral interview test. You have already taken the written test and you are now being called for the interview test – the final part of the formal examination.

You may think that it is not possible to prepare for an interview test and that there are no procedures to follow during an interview. Our purpose is to point out some things you can do in advance that will help you and some good rules to follow and pitfalls to avoid while you are being interviewed.

What is an interview supposed to test?

The written examination is designed to test the technical knowledge and competence of the candidate; the oral is designed to evaluate intangible qualities, not readily measured otherwise, and to establish a list showing the relative fitness of each candidate – as measured against his competitors – for the position sought. Scoring is not on the basis of "right" and "wrong," but on a sliding scale of values ranging from "not passable" to "outstanding." As a matter of fact, it is possible to achieve a relatively low score without a single "incorrect" answer because of evident weakness in the qualities being measured.

Occasionally, an examination may consist entirely of an oral test – either an individual or a group oral. In such cases, information is sought concerning the technical knowledges and abilities of the candidate, since there has been no written examination for this purpose. More commonly, however, an oral test is used to supplement a written examination.

Who conducts interviews?

The composition of oral boards varies among different jurisdictions. In nearly all, a representative of the personnel department serves as chairman. One of the members of the board may be a representative of the department in which the candidate would work. In some cases, "outside experts" are used, and, frequently, a businessman or some other representative of the general public is asked to serve. Labor and management or other special groups may be represented. The aim is to secure the services of experts in the appropriate field.

However the board is composed, it is a good idea (and not at all improper or unethical) to ascertain in advance of the interview who the members are and what groups they represent. When you are introduced to them, you will have some idea of their backgrounds and interests, and at least you will not stutter and stammer over their names.

What should be done before the interview?

While knowledge about the board members is useful and takes some of the surprise element out of the interview, there is other preparation which is more substantive. It *is* possible to prepare for an oral interview – in several ways:

1) Keep a copy of your application and review it carefully before the interview

This may be the only document before the oral board, and the starting point of the interview. Know what education and experience you have listed there, and the sequence and dates of all of it. Sometimes the board will ask you to review the highlights of your experience for them; you should not have to hem and haw doing it.

2) Study the class specification and the examination announcement

Usually, the oral board has one or both of these to guide them. The qualities, characteristics or knowledges required by the position sought are stated in these documents. They offer valuable clues as to the nature of the oral interview. For example, if the job involves supervisory responsibilities, the announcement will usually indicate that knowledge of modern supervisory methods and the qualifications of the candidate as a supervisor will be tested. If so, you can expect such questions, frequently in the form of a hypothetical situation which you are expected to solve. NEVER go into an oral without knowledge of the duties and responsibilities of the job you seek.

3) Think through each qualification required

Try to visualize the kind of questions you would ask if you were a board member. How well could you answer them? Try especially to appraise your own knowledge and background in each area, *measured against the job sought*, and identify any areas in which you are weak. Be critical and realistic – do not flatter yourself.

4) Do some general reading in areas in which you feel you may be weak

For example, if the job involves supervision and your past experience has NOT, some general reading in supervisory methods and practices, particularly in the field of human relations, might be useful. Do NOT study agency procedures or detailed manuals. The oral board will be testing your understanding and capacity, not your memory.

5) Get a good night's sleep and watch your general health and mental attitude

You will want a clear head at the interview. Take care of a cold or any other minor ailment, and of course, no hangovers.

What should be done on the day of the interview?

Now comes the day of the interview itself. Give yourself plenty of time to get there. Plan to arrive somewhat ahead of the scheduled time, particularly if your appointment is in the fore part of the day. If a previous candidate fails to appear, the board might be ready for you a bit early. By early afternoon an oral board is almost invariably behind schedule if there are many candidates, and you may have to wait. Take along a book or magazine to read, or your application to review, but leave any extraneous material in the waiting room when you go in for your interview. In any event, relax and compose yourself.

The matter of dress is important. The board is forming impressions about you – from your experience, your manners, your attitude, and your appearance. Give your personal appearance careful attention. Dress your best, but not your flashiest. Choose conservative, appropriate clothing, and be sure it is immaculate. This is a business interview, and your appearance should indicate that you regard it as such. Besides, being well groomed and properly dressed will help boost your confidence.

Sooner or later, someone will call your name and escort you into the interview room. *This is it.* From here on you are on your own. It is too late for any more preparation. But remember, you asked for this opportunity to prove your fitness, and you are here because your request was granted.

What happens when you go in?

The usual sequence of events will be as follows: The clerk (who is often the board stenographer) will introduce you to the chairman of the oral board, who will introduce you to the other members of the board. Acknowledge the introductions before you sit down. Do not be surprised if you find a microphone facing you or a stenotypist sitting by. Oral interviews are usually recorded in the event of an appeal or other review.

Usually the chairman of the board will open the interview by reviewing the highlights of your education and work experience from your application – primarily for the benefit of the other members of the board, as well as to get the material into the record. Do not interrupt or comment unless there is an error or significant misinterpretation; if that is the case, do not hesitate. But do not quibble about insignificant matters. Also, he will usually ask you some question about your education, experience or your present job – partly to get you to start talking and to establish the interviewing "rapport." He may start the actual questioning, or turn it over to one of the other members. Frequently, each member undertakes the questioning on a particular area, one in which he is perhaps most competent, so you can expect each member to participate in the examination. Because time is limited, you may also expect some rather abrupt switches in the direction the questioning takes, so do not be upset by it. Normally, a board member will not pursue a single line of questioning unless he discovers a particular strength or weakness.

After each member has participated, the chairman will usually ask whether any member has any further questions, then will ask you if you have anything you wish to add. Unless you are expecting this question, it may floor you. Worse, it may start you off on an extended, extemporaneous speech. The board is not usually seeking more information. The question is principally to offer you a last opportunity to present further qualifications or to indicate that you have nothing to add. So, if you feel that a significant qualification or characteristic has been overlooked, it is proper to point it out in a sentence or so. Do not compliment the board on the thoroughness of their examination – they have been sketchy, and you know it. If you wish, merely say, "No thank you, I have nothing further to add." This is a point where you can "talk yourself out" of a good impression or fail to present an important bit of information. Remember, *you close the interview yourself*.

The chairman will then say, "That is all, Mr. _____, thank you." Do not be startled; the interview is over, and quicker than you think. Thank him, gather your belongings and take your leave. Save your sigh of relief for the other side of the door.

How to put your best foot forward

Throughout this entire process, you may feel that the board individually and collectively is trying to pierce your defenses, seek out your hidden weaknesses and embarrass and confuse you. Actually, this is not true. They are obliged to make an appraisal of your qualifications for the job you are seeking, and they want to see you in your best light. Remember, they must interview all candidates and a non-cooperative candidate may become a failure in spite of their best efforts to bring out his qualifications. Here are 15 suggestions that will help you:

1) Be natural – Keep your attitude confident, not cocky

If you are not confident that you can do the job, do not expect the board to be. Do not apologize for your weaknesses, try to bring out your strong points. The board is interested in a positive, not negative, presentation. Cockiness will antagonize any board member and make him wonder if you are covering up a weakness by a false show of strength.

2) Get comfortable, but don't lounge or sprawl

Sit erectly but not stiffly. A careless posture may lead the board to conclude that you are careless in other things, or at least that you are not impressed by the importance of the occasion. Either conclusion is natural, even if incorrect. Do not fuss with your clothing, a pencil or an ashtray. Your hands may occasionally be useful to emphasize a point; do not let them become a point of distraction.

3) Do not wisecrack or make small talk

This is a serious situation, and your attitude should show that you consider it as such. Further, the time of the board is limited – they do not want to waste it, and neither should you.

4) Do not exaggerate your experience or abilities

In the first place, from information in the application or other interviews and sources, the board may know more about you than you think. Secondly, you probably will not get away with it. An experienced board is rather adept at spotting such a situation, so do not take the chance.

5) If you know a board member, do not make a point of it, yet do not hide it

Certainly you are not fooling him, and probably not the other members of the board. Do not try to take advantage of your acquaintanceship – it will probably do you little good.

6) Do not dominate the interview

Let the board do that. They will give you the clues – do not assume that you have to do all the talking. Realize that the board has a number of questions to ask you, and do not try to take up all the interview time by showing off your extensive knowledge of the answer to the first one.

7) Be attentive

You only have 20 minutes or so, and you should keep your attention at its sharpest throughout. When a member is addressing a problem or question to you, give him your undivided attention. Address your reply principally to him, but do not exclude the other board members.

8) Do not interrupt

A board member may be stating a problem for you to analyze. He will ask you a question when the time comes. Let him state the problem, and wait for the question.

9) Make sure you understand the question

Do not try to answer until you are sure what the question is. If it is not clear, restate it in your own words or ask the board member to clarify it for you. However, do not haggle about minor elements.

10) Reply promptly but not hastily

A common entry on oral board rating sheets is "candidate responded readily," or "candidate hesitated in replies." Respond as promptly and quickly as you can, but do not jump to a hasty, ill-considered answer.

11) Do not be peremptory in your answers

A brief answer is proper – but do not fire your answer back. That is a losing game from your point of view. The board member can probably ask questions much faster than you can answer them.

12) Do not try to create the answer you think the board member wants

He is interested in what kind of mind you have and how it works – not in playing games. Furthermore, he can usually spot this practice and will actually grade you down on it.

13) Do not switch sides in your reply merely to agree with a board member

Frequently, a member will take a contrary position merely to draw you out and to see if you are willing and able to defend your point of view. Do not start a debate, yet do not surrender a good position. If a position is worth taking, it is worth defending.

14) Do not be afraid to admit an error in judgment if you are shown to be wrong

The board knows that you are forced to reply without any opportunity for careful consideration. Your answer may be demonstrably wrong. If so, admit it and get on with the interview.

15) Do not dwell at length on your present job

The opening question may relate to your present assignment. Answer the question but do not go into an extended discussion. You are being examined for a *new* job, not your present one. As a matter of fact, try to phrase ALL your answers in terms of the job for which you are being examined.

Basis of Rating

Probably you will forget most of these "do's" and "don'ts" when you walk into the oral interview room. Even remembering them all will not ensure you a passing grade. Perhaps you did not have the qualifications in the first place. But remembering them will help you to put your best foot forward, without treading on the toes of the board members.

Rumor and popular opinion to the contrary notwithstanding, an oral board wants you to make the best appearance possible. They know you are under pressure – but they also want to see how you respond to it as a guide to what your reaction would be under the pressures of the job you seek. They will be influenced by the degree of poise you display, the personal traits you show and the manner in which you respond.

ABOUT THIS BOOK

This book contains tests divided into Examination Sections. Go through each test, answering every question in the margin. We have also attached a sample answer sheet at the back of the book that can be removed and used. At the end of each test look at the answer key and check your answers. On the ones you got wrong, look at the right answer choice and learn. Do not fill in the answers first. Do not memorize the questions and answers, but understand the answer and principles involved. On your test, the questions will likely be different from the samples. Questions are changed and new ones added. If you understand these past questions you should have success with any changes that arise. Tests may consist of several types of questions. We have additional books on each subject should more study be advisable or necessary for you. Finally, the more you study, the better prepared you will be. This book is intended to be the last thing you study before you walk into the examination room. Prior study of relevant texts is also recommended. NLC publishes some of these in our Fundamental Series. Knowledge and good sense are important factors in passing your exam. Good luck also helps. So now study this Passbook, absorb the material contained within and take that knowledge into the examination. Then do your best to pass that exam.

EXAMINATION SECTION

EXAMINATION SECTION
TEST 1

DIRECTIONS: Each question or incomplete statement is followed by several suggested answers or completions. Select the one that BEST answers the question or completes the statement. *PRINT THE LETTER OF THE CORRECT ANSWER IN THE SPACE AT THE RIGHT.*

1. The one of the following that is NOT a responsibility of a bridge operator is

    A. having the roadways properly sanded when necessary during his shift
    B. having snow and debris swept from all bridge property during his shift
    C. inspection of searchlights at least once during his shift
    D. reporting the time of inspections of the structure on his shift in the log book

    1.____

2. The visual signal given by the bridge operator at night that the draw will be opened IMMEDIATELY is a _____ light swung _____ several times in full sight of the vessel.

    A. white; to and fro horizontally
    B. white; up and down vertically
    C. green; to and fro horizontally
    D. green; up and down vertically

    2.____

3. The bridge operator shall see that the bridge is patrolled by at least

    A. one man at all times
    B. one man, once each shift
    C. one man, twice each shift
    D. two men, once each shift

    3.____

4. The bridge operator should inspect all electrical lighting and signal equipment on his bridge

    A. once each shift   B. twice each day
    C. every week   D. three times a week

    4.____

5. When a large vessel and a small vessel are approaching to pass a drawbridge from opposite directions, the one HAVING the right of way at slack tide is the

    A. vessel closer to the drawbridge
    B. larger vessel
    C. vessel running in the direction of the ebb current
    D. smaller vessel

    5.____

6. The sound signals to be given by a vessel to indicate that the draw should be OPENED is _____ blasts of a whistle or horn.

    A. five   B. four
    C. three   D. two

    6.____

7. Accidents which cause a delay in traffic are to be reported by telephone to the section office and supervisor if the delay is _____ minutes or more.

    A. 10   B. 15
    C. 20   D. 30

    7.____

1

8. Assume that a tug with a tall smokestack is towing two flat, fully loaded barges through the draw.
   The bridge operator may start to close the draw when the

   A. barge which is at the rear has completely cleared the draw
   B. tall smokestack of the tug is clear of the draw
   C. stern of the tug cleared the draw
   D. bow of the tug has cleared the draw

9. Assume that a tug and a tug towing a barge are approaching to pass a drawbridge from opposite directions.
   The one HAVING the right of way is the

   A. tug
   B. tug towing the barge
   C. vessel running against the current
   D. vessel running with the current

10. Visual signals should be used whenever sound signals cannot be given or if sound signals cannot be heard.
    The signals are PRESCRIBED by the Department of

    A. the Navy
    B. the Army
    C. the Coast Guard
    D. Commerce

11. The visual signal to be used at night by a vessel requesting the opening of a draw is a white light swung _____ in full sight of the bridge and facing the draw.

    A. up and down vertically a number of times
    B. from side to side horizontally a number of times
    C. in full circles at arm's length
    D. in half circles at arm's length

12. The bridge should promptly answer all call signals from a vessel for opening the draw by blowing _____ blasts of a whistle.

    A. four
    B. three
    C. two
    D. one long

13. The visual signal to be used by the bridge operator at *night* to indicate that the draw CANNOT be opened immediately is a _____ light swung _____ in full sight of the vessel.

    A. white; in full circles at arm's length
    B. white; up and down vertically a number of times
    C. red; up and down vertically a number of times
    D. red; to and fro horizontally

14. The signal, given by the bridge operator and repeated at regular intervals until acknowledged by the vessel, that the draw is open and must be closed IMMEDIATELY is _____ long blast(s) of a whistle or horn.

    A. one; followed by a short blast of a whistle or horn
    B. two
    C. three
    D. four

15. The signal given by the bridge operator to a vessel when the draw is FULLY opened is   15.____

    A. the same as the call signal
    B. one long blast of a whistle or horn
    C. two long blasts of a whistle or horn
    D. three short blasts of a whistle or horn

16. Due to mechanical or electrical trouble the draw cannot be closed. In the opinion of the   16.____
    bridge operator a long delay is probable.
    Of the following, the agency to notify *after* contacting the supervisor and section office
    is the

    A. Department of the Army   B. Coast Guard
    C. Fire Department   D. Sanitation Department

17. The one of the following duties which is NOT a responsibility of the bridge operator is   17.____

    A. inspecting fire extinguishers
    B. entering structural defects to machinery in the log
    C. signing the daily time sheets
    D. preparing all accident reports on his shift

18. The type of friction brake operated by a motor which builds up pressure in an oil drum   18.____
    and causes a cylinder inside to move upwards, thus releasing the brake, is called a
    _____ brake.

    A. thrustor motor   B. disk
    C. magnetic   D. band

19. The type of bridge on which a skew indicator is used MOST frequently is a _____   19.____
    bridge.

    A. lift   B. swing
    C. retractile   D. bascule

20. The one of the following that is considered a dead load is a   20.____

    A. bridge leaf   B. snow load
    C. wind load   D. moving vehicle

21. The type of bridge on which a trunnion is used is the _____ bridge.   21.____

    A. vertical lift   B. bascule
    C. swing   D. retractile

22. The material of which buffer blocks are made is USUALLY   22.____

    A. steel   B. wood
    C. iron   D. brass

23. From the closed position to the nearly closed position on the controller, for a bascule   23.____
    bridge, only the FIRST _____ power points are available.

    A. three   B. four
    C. five   D. six

24. When the controller for a bascule bridge is raised to first power point 1 - Raise, 24.____

   A. the shaft brakes will automatically be released
   B. power will be applied to the motors
   C. the motor brakes will automatically be released
   D. the motors will accelerate to the fourth point in automatic steps controlled by a timer

25. When the controller for a bascule bridge is moved to the second and third B-Raise position, the 25.____

   A. motor brakes will be released
   B. shaft brakes will be released
   C. motors will automatically decelerate
   D. shear locks will automatically open

26. When the controller is set to the first B-Raise position, the 26.____

   A. oncoming barriers will automatically be lowered
   B. shaft brakes will be released
   C. the shear locks will automatically open
   D. motor brakes will be locked

27. Once the traffic lights on a swing bridge are on and the roadway gates are closed, the sequence of operations is: 27.____

   A. Release end wedges, unlatch span, release of centre wedges, and operate span
   B. Unlatch span, release end wedges, release centre wedges, and operate span
   C. Release centre wedges, unlatch span, operate span and release end wedges
   D. Unlatch span, release centre wedges, release end wedges, and operate span

28. The one of the following which is a type of swing bridge is the _____ bridge. 28.____

   A. Scherzer   B. center bearing
   C. Rall   D. Strauss

29. Of the following, the type of motor that is *best* to use when high starting torque is required and the speed variation is large and NOT objectionable, is the _____ motor. 29.____

   A. shunt   B. series
   C. compound   D. split-phase

30. Resistance of an electrical circuit may be DIRECTLY measured by using a(n) 30.____

   A. ohmmeter   B. ammeter   C. voltmeter   D. wattmeter

31. A device used to change a low d.c. voltage to a high d.c. voltage is a 31.____

   A. rectifier   B. dynamotor
   C. transformer   D. coil

32. The device which does NOT operate automatically to protect a circuit on an overload is a 32.____

   A. ballast resistor   B. relay
   C. circuit breaker   D. fuse

33. An instrument used for measuring electrical power is a(n)

    A. voltmeter
    B. power factor meter
    C. ammeter
    D. wattmeter

34. The device used to raise or lower the available a.c. voltage is a

    A. relay
    B. transformer
    C. rectifier
    D. capacitor

35. The nominal voltage, in volts, of a lead acid storage battery having six cells is

    A. 24   B. 18   C. 12   D. 6

36. Assume that the fuse of a certain lighting circuit in the bridge house burns out and the circuit must be restored to service. A fuse with the same rating is not available.
    The FIRST thing to do is to

    A. call the electrician to check the circuit
    B. replace the fuse with one that has a higher rating
    C. replace the fuse with one that has a lower rating
    D. replace the fuse with a copper bar

37. The device that shuts off power to the motor when the leaf of a bascule bridge reaches the end of its travel is a(n)

    A. limit switch
    B. time switch
    C. over-voltage relay
    D. overload relay

38. The speed of a wound rotor induction motor may be INCREASED by

    A. *increasing* the series field resistance
    B. *decreasing* the shunt field resistance
    C. *decreasing* the rotor circuit resistance
    D. *increasing* the shunt field current

39. The device which keeps an electrical contactor from operating too rapidly is a

    A. limit switch
    B. start-stop switch
    C. overload relay
    D. dash-pot

40. Whenever the drawbridge is opened for a vessel, the bridge operator is required to record certain information.
    The one of the following that is NOT recorded by the bridge operator when he opens a draw is the

    A. time of the opening
    B. name of the vessel
    C. type of vessel
    D. tonnage of the vessel

41. The one of the following items that is recorded in the log book is the

    A. number of vehicles crossing the bridge
    B. number of emergency vehicles crossing the bridge
    C. times that emergency vehicles cross the bridge
    D. number of boats passing under the bridge with draw closed

42. The time of an opening of the draw which is entered in the log is the

    A. interval between the time the vessel first starts to pass under the draw and the time when the vessel has cleared the draw
    B. interval between the time the traffic gates are closed and the time they are opened
    C. time when the vessel first starts to pass under the draw
    D. time when the vessel has cleared the draw

43. Accidents are to be *reported* to the _____ office on "Accident Report Form _____."

    A. section; A-17
    B. section; A70
    C. main; A 17
    D. main; A70

44. The log book must be kept on the top of the desk for ready reference by the

    A. assistant bridge operators
    B. bridge operator on duty
    C. bridge operator-in-charge
    D. officials of the department

45. The upper portion of each page of the log book should be divided into

    A. two parts   B. three parts
    C. four parts   D. as many parts as needed

KEY (CORRECT ANSWERS)

1. C	11. C	21. B	31. B	41. D
2. D	12. C	22. B	32. A	42. B
3. A	13. D	23. B	33. D	43. B
4. A	14. B	24. B	34. B	44. D
5. C	15. A	25. A	35. C	45. B
6. B	16. C	26. B	36. C	
7. D	17. A	27. A	37. A	
8. A	18. A	28. B	38. C	
9. D	19. A	29. B	39. D	
10. B	20. A	30. A	40. D	

TEST 2

DIRECTIONS: Each question or incomplete statement is followed by several suggested answers or completions. Select the one that BEST answers the question or completes the statement. *PRINT THE LETTER OF THE CORRECT ANSWER IN THE SPACE AT THE RIGHT.*

1. In determining whether to discipline an assistant bridge operator, the bridge operator should consider

    A. the opinions of the assistant bridge operator's fellow workers
    B. his current salary
    C. his age
    D. the quality of his general performance

2. The one of the following actions which a bridge operator can take in order to maintain good morale among his subordinates is to

    A. give instructions indirectly
    B. encourage cliques, thereby building a spirit of good fellowship
    C. concern himself with his subordinates' personal problems
    D. always have an excuse for his mistakes

3. Assume that one of your assistant bridge operators comes to you with a grievance. The one of the following which you should NOT do is

    A. tell him to talk to you in private
    B. let the assistant talk as much as he wants
    C. have a violent argument with the assistant
    D. listen to him sympathetically

4. Assume that you are a bridge operator and that one of the assistant bridge operators on your shift, who has always been very punctual, begins to arrive late fairly often. The FIRST action that you should take after you have noticed this pattern of lateness is to

    A. *bawl* him out
    B. tell him he will get all the *dirty work* if he keeps on being late
    C. threaten to bring him up on charges
    D. talk to him to see if you can determine the reason why he is late so often

5. Of the following, the BEST approach to use to secure cooperation from assistant bridge operators working under your supervision is to

    A. be a stern disciplinarian at all times
    B. let the men use their own judgment at all times
    C. listen to the men's problems and help them where possible
    D. support the men whenever they have a complaint

6. A bridge operator should instruct his assistant bridge operators to treat the public with

    A. disdain
    B. disinterest
    C. aloofness
    D. courtesy

7. If a bridge operator makes a mistake in giving instructions to his assistant bridge operators, he should

   A. find reasons to defend his actions
   B. first determine whether the error is a major one before deciding on his course of action
   C. admit his error and correct the instructions
   D. ignore the error, since the men will do the job properly as soon as they discover the mistake

7.____

8. Suggestions concerning working conditions made by newly appointed assistant bridge operators should be

   A. *encouraged* because the suggestions may be good ones
   B. *encouraged* because these men have better ideas than the older workers
   C. *discouraged* because these men have little experience
   D. *discouraged* because the suggestions waste too much of the bridge operators' time

8.____

9. Assume that a bridge operator sees one of his assistant bridge operators doing a job incorrectly.
   The BEST course of action for the bridge operator to take is to

   A. scold the assistant bridge operator
   B. threaten the assistant bridge operator with disciplinary action
   C. tell the assistant bridge operator exactly how to do the job properly
   D. bring the assistant bridge operator up on charges

9.____

10. In order to improve the safety record of the assistant bridge operators, a bridge operator should discourage

    A. tardiness
    C. horseplay
    B. absenteeism
    D. malingering

10.____

11. Assume that two of your assistant bridge operators are working together and that you notice one of them breaking a department rule.
    The PROPER course of action for you to take is

    A. to *bawl* the man out immediately for breaking the rules
    B. call both men into your office, quote the rule to them and tell them to observe it in the future
    C. speak to the man who broke the rule in private, reprimanding him for the action
    D. threaten the man who broke the rule with disciplinary action

11.____

12. When a bridge operator has confidence in his assistant bridge operators, he

    A. must still provide adequate supervision
    B. must be more careful than usual in supervising the assistant bridge operators
    C. need not supervise their work
    D. can delegate supervision to one of his assistant bridge operators

12.____

13. Of the following, a *reliable* employee is one who

    A. is argumentative
    C. gets along with his fellow workers
    B. learns quickly
    D. needs little supervision

13.____

14. A bridge operator wants his assistant bridge operators to be able to operate the draw in case of an emergency. Of the following, the BEST approach for the bridge operator to take to attain this objective would be to give the men

    A. time off to learn the procedure
    B. written instructions on how to operate the draw
    C. oral instructions on how to operate the draw
    D. actual operating experience under the direct supervision of the bridge operator

15. One important use of accident reports is to provide information that may be used to reduce the possibility of similar accidents.
    The MOST important entry for this purpose on an accident report made out by a bridge operator is the

    A. location of the accident
    B. cause of the accident
    C. injury sustained by the victim
    D. name of the victim

16. Class C fire extinguishers should be used on burning

    A. wood or paper
    B. oil
    C. electrical wiring
    D. magnesium or potassium

17. Of the following, the BEST location for storing wooden ladders is

    A. near radiators
    B. near steam pipes
    C. in damp basements
    D. in ventilated rooms

18. Of the following, the MAIN reason for NOT using water to extinguish fires in or around electrical equipment is that the water could

    A. corrode the electrical conductors
    B. cause the circuit fuses to blow
    C. damage the insulation
    D. conduct electrical current and may cause shock

19. Of the following, the action that is MOST likely to have the GREATEST effect in improving safety is

    A. posting numerous safety bulletins
    B. holding the bridge operator accountable for accidents caused by assistant bridge operators
    C. periodic safety inspections
    D. providing each assistant bridge operator with periodic safety notices

20. Of the following, the SAFEST type of can to use for storing oil soaked rags indoors is a

    A. plastic container with a plastic cover
    B. plastic container without a cover
    C. sheet metal can with a perforated sheet metal cover
    D. sheet metal can with a solid sheet metal cover

21. If a fluid is to be administered to a person suffering from shock who is conscious, the BEST fluid to use is

    A. lukewarm water
    B. an alcoholic drink
    C. hot coffee
    D. cold tea

22. Compensator time earned by employees MUST be used within _____ days from the date of accrual.

    A. 90
    B. 120
    C. 180
    D. 365

23. An employee desiring time off to observe a religious holy day should submit a request form for such leave at LEAST _____ days in advance of the holy day.

    A. three
    B. five
    C. seven
    D. ten

24. The one of the following that is excused without charge to either sick leave or annual leave is an absence due to

    A. aggravation of a disability originally incurred in the armed forces
    B. attendance in court for jury duty
    C. attendance in court when the absentee is suing another party
    D. an automobile accident

25. The number of days of annual leave that may be used for personal business and/or religious holidays is

    A. five
    B. seven
    C. ten
    D. twelve

5 (#2)

KEY (CORRECT ANSWERS)

1. D
2. C
3. C
4. D
5. C

6. D
7. C
8. A
9. C
10. C

11. C
12. A
13. D
14. D
15. B

16. C
17. D
18. D
19. C
20. D

21. A
22. A
23. D
24. B
25. B

———

EXAMINATION SECTION
TEST 1

DIRECTIONS: Each question or incomplete statement is followed by several suggested answers or completions. Select the one that BEST answers the question or completes the statement. *PRINT THE LETTER OF THE CORRECT ANSWER IN THE SPACE AT THE RIGHT.*

1. Electrical energy is measured with a(n) 1._____

   A. ammeter
   B. phase meter
   C. watt meter
   D. watt hour meter

2. To change A.C. current to D.C. current, it is required to use a 2._____

   A. rectifier
   B. transformer
   C. choke coil
   D. condenser

3. The A.C. motor that uses external secondary circuit resistance for proper operation is COMMONLY called a _____ motor. 3._____

   A. squirrel cage induction
   B. wound rotor induction
   C. repulsion
   D. split phase

4. A constantly dropping barometer reading is an indication of 4._____

   A. an approaching storm
   B. an approaching cold wave
   C. forthcoming good weather
   D. an extremely low tide

5. A boat that weighs 15 tons has a displacement of MOST NEARLY _____ tons. 5._____

   A. 5   B. 10   C. 15   D. 20

6. The periodic rise and fall of the waters of the ocean and its inlets is due to the 6._____

   A. changes in weather
   B. atmospheric conditions
   C. gaseous fluid surrounding the earth
   D. attraction of the moon and sun

7. The Ninth Street Bridge is a _____ bridge. 7._____

   A. Scherzer bascule
   B. skew bascule
   C. lift
   D. retractile

8. The Third Avenue (Harlem) Bridge is a _____ bridge. 8._____

   A. Scherzer bascule
   B. swing
   C. lift
   D. retractile

9. If part of a walkway measuring 9 feet by 20 feet is to be replaced by concrete 6 inches thick, the cubic yards of concrete needed is MOST NEARLY 9._____

   A. $1\frac{1}{2}$ B. $3\frac{1}{2}$ C. 42   D. 90

10. The one of the following which is BEST suited to test the electrolyte of a battery is a(n) 10._____

   A. manometer B. hydrometer
   C. electrometer D. hygrometer

11. Continuity of the conductors in an electrical circuit can be determined by means of a 11._____

   A. bell and battery set B. Preece test
   C. rectifier D. potentiometer

12. On a swing-type drawbridge, the 12._____

   A. locks are located at each end of the swing
   B. counterweights are located at the end of the span
   C. locks are located in the middle of the span
   D. counterweights are located in the middle of the span

13. If a cartridge fuse slip makes contact with the fuse with much less than normal spring tension, the result would MOST likely be that the 13._____

   A. fuse will immediately burn out
   B. voltage at the supply will be high
   C. voltage at the load will be high
   D. clips will become warm

14. A device commonly used to step down voltage of an A.C. source of supply is called a 14._____

   A. choke coil B. relay
   C. contactor D. transformer

15. Electrical power is measured with a(n) 15._____

   A. ammeter B. voltmeter
   C. wattmeter D. galvanometer

16. Electrical current is conveniently measured with a(n) 16._____

   A. ammeter B. voltmeter C. wattmeter D. ohmmeter

17. Potential difference is measured with a(n) 17._____

   A. ammeter B. voltmeter C. wattmeter D. ohmmeter

18. The side of a boat to the right of a person standing on deck and looking towards the bow is called 18._____

   A. port B. starboard C. chine D. transom

19. A recess aft, in the deck of a boat, which provides a small amount of deck space at a lower level is called 19._____

   A. garvey B. hatch pit C. cock pit D. keelson

20. Assume that a sump pit measures 10 feet long, 10 feet wide, and 12 feet deep. If each cubic foot of water is equal to 7.5 gallons, the amount of water in the sump when half full will be MOST NEARLY _____ gallons. 20._____

   A. 120 B. 1,200 C. 4,500 D. 9,000

21. If the water in a sump pit is 10 feet deep, the pressure at the bottom of the pit, in lbs. per sq. in. exerted by the water, is MOST NEARLY (assuming water weighs 62.4 lbs./cu.ft.)

    A. 4.3 B. 52 C. 62.4 D. 624

21.____

22. In order to automatically stop the bridge motor when the bridge leaf reaches the end of its travel, it is necessary to incorporate into the control circuit a(n) _____ switch.

    A. limit
    B. astronomical
    C. electronic
    D. rotary

22.____

23. In a gasoline engine, the part that most likely prevents the crankcase lubricating oil from getting into the combustion chamber is MOST likely the

    A. compression pressure in the cylinder
    B. piston ring
    C. oil filter
    D. splash skirt

23.____

24. Assume that the auxiliary bridge gasoline engine will not start even though the gasoline tank is 3/4 full and a good spark is present at the plugs. The FIRST logical thing to do is to

    A. check the battery
    B. test the distributor
    C. test if gasoline is being delivered to the carburetor
    D. check the oil

24.____

25. Assume that the fuse of a 208 volt two-wire power circuit blew. Assume that with the switch in the opened position, one of the probes of a test lamp set is placed on the live side of the switch and the other probe on the circuit side of the switch. If the lamps light up, this is an indication that the circuit is

    A. shorted
    B. open
    C. overloaded
    D. grounded

25.____

26. According to the departmental rules on accidents, incidents and delays to traffic, which state that if, because of mechanical or electrical trouble, the draw cannot be opened, or, if opened, it cannot be closed and in the opinion of the bridge operator a long delay is possible, the BEST course of action the operator should take is to notify the police department,

    A. the main office, and the United States engineers' office
    B. and the fire department before notifying the main office, the section office, and the United States engineers' office
    C. and fire department after notifying the main office and the sectional office
    D. fire department, United States engineers' office before notifying the main office and the sectional office

26.____

27. According to the departmental rules on opening of a bridge, the time of an opening should be the interval

    A. during which the draw is fully open
    B. between the time the draw begins to open and the time it is fully closed again

27.____

C. between the time the traffic gates are closed and the time they are opened
D. between the answering of the call signal for the opening and the signal to open all the traffic gates

28. Assume that a vessel with a tow and one without a tow are approaching to pass the drawbridge from opposite directions. The vessel which has the right-of-way is the one

    A. which signaled first
    B. with the tow
    C. running with the current
    D. without a tow

29. Unless A.C. motors use proper starting equipment, during starting period, it is likely that the motor will

    A. draw a comparatively low current
    B. draw a comparatively high current
    C. have a tendency to overspeed
    D. not run in the proper direction

30. Brakes are used to stop and hold the bridge span. It can be CORRECTLY stated that quick setting brakes for bridge work are

    A. *not desirable,* because they would bring the span to an abrupt stop
    B. *desirable,* because of their smooth operation
    C. *desirable,* because they are faster acting
    D. *not desirable,* because of the strain put on the main motors

31. Assume that a gear and pinion combination have a ratio of 3 to 1. If the gear should rotate at 150 revolutions per minute, the speed of the pinion, in revolutions per minute, would be MOST NEARLY

    A. 30   B. 90   C. 150   D. 450

32. Assume that the bridge operator may at times be assigned to the task of coordinating the bridge crew for the various routine jobs.
    In the above sentence, the word coordinating means MOST NEARLY

    A. ordering
    B. testing
    C. scheduling
    D. instructing

33. Protective devices for bridge piers and similar structures over navigable waters are USUALLY called

    A. fenders   B. bulkheads   C. docks   D. levees

34. A number of closely driven piles that are wrapped together at the top are called a

    A. jetty group
    B. dolphin cluster
    C. timber groin
    D. pile crib

35. In the statement, *The bridge operator made an insignificant error,* the word insignificant means MOST NEARLY

    A. latent
    B. serious
    C. accidental
    D. minor

KEY (CORRECT ANSWERS)

1. D
2. A
3. B
4. A
5. C

6. D
7. A
8. B
9. B
10. B

11. A
12. A
13. D
14. D
15. C

16. A
17. B
18. B
19. C
20. C

21. A
22. A
23. B
24. C
25. D

26. C
27. C
28. C
29. B
30. A

31. D
32. C
33. A
34. B
35. D

———

TEST 2

DIRECTIONS: Each question or incomplete statement is followed by several suggested answers or completions. Select the one that BEST answers the question or completes the statement. *PRINT THE LETTER OF THE CORRECT ANSWER IN THE SPACE AT THE RIGHT.*

1. Assume that you are a bridge operator, and orders which will be unpopular with your men are to be posted on your bulletin board. Of the following, your BEST course of action is to

    A. tell the men that you disagree with the orders
    B. call the men together and advise them to protest the orders
    C. tell the men that you will try to get the orders changed
    D. post the orders without comment

2. A defect in the structure is discovered by an assistant bridge operator. The rules of the department require that this condition be

    A. recorded in the log by the assistant bridge operator who discovered it
    B. recorded in the log by the bridge operator-in-charge
    C. reported to the main office
    D. recorded in the log by the bridge operator and be reported to the bridge operator-in-charge

3. Accident reports should be filled out by the

    A. assistant bridge operator who witnessed the accident
    B. bridge operator-in-charge
    C. bridge operator on duty
    D. supervisor of bridge operation

4. Assume that you are a bridge operator and that one day you notice two assistant bridge operators who are working near each other but on different jobs. One of these men is lax about his work.
   Your CORRECT course of action is

    A. to ignore the lax worker and go about your business
    B. *bawl out* the lax worker on the spot
    C. take the lax worker aside and reprimand him in private
    D. take over the job of the lax worker and show him how it should be done

5. According to the River and Harbor Act, a bridge operator who *wilfully refuses or fails to open or cause to be opened the draw of a bridge* in accordance with the regulations shall be

    A. deemed guilty of a felony
    B. deemed guilty of misconduct
    C. reprimanded
    D. deemed guilty of a misdemeanor

6. By night, the visual call signal made by a vessel for the opening of the draw when sound equipment is out of order is a _____ light swung _____ in full sight of the bridge and facing the draw.

    A. white; from side to side a number of times
    B. white; in complete circles at arms length
    C. green; up and down a number of times
    D. green; in complete circles at arms length

7. When conditions are such that sound signals cannot be heard, by day, the visual signal from the bridge indicating that the draw is to be opened immediately is a _____ flag swung _____ in full sight of the vessel.

    A. red; to and fro horizontally
    B. white; to and fro horizontally
    C. red; up and down vertically a number of times
    D. white; up and down vertically a number of times

8. Assume that sound equipment on a vessel is out of order. At night, this vessel signals, by means of a light, for the opening of the draw. The bridge signals back that the draw cannot be opened immediately. The vessel will CORRECTLY acknowledge the received signal by swinging a _____ light _____.

    A. red; to and fro horizontally
    B. white; to and fro horizontally
    C. red; up and down vertically
    D. white; up and down vertically

9. Of the following delays that might be caused by accidents, the one which should IMMEDIATELY be reported by telephone to the section or main office is the delay from

    A. 11:45 P.M. to 12:10 A.M.
    B. 1:10 A.M. to 1:30 A.M.
    C. 11:50 P.M. to 12:20 A.M.
    D. 2:10 P.M. to 2:35 P.M.

10. When closing the bridge span, the sequence of operation MUST be so interlocked that before the locks or wedges are driven the

    A. bridge is moved laterally
    B. span is seated
    C. traffic barrier or gates are opened
    D. electric power must be shut off

11. The proper sequence of operation when opening a bridge is to FIRST

    A. withdraw the bridge locks or wedges
    B. move the span leaves slowly
    C. stop the traffic across the bridge
    D. release all motor brakes

12. A knot which is used to safely join together two ropes of different sizes is GENERALLY called a _____ knot.

    A. square   B. crown   C. wall   D. sheet bend

13. The acknowledging sound signal used by the bridge operator to indicate to a boat that the call signal has been heard and that preparations to open the bridge will be made is MOST likely

    A. 2 loud and distinct strokes of a bell
    B. 3 loud and distinct strokes of a bell
    C. 4 loud and distinct strokes of a bell
    D. one more stroke of the bell than given in the call signal

14. According to *Rules and Regulations Governing the Opening of Drawbridges in Conformity with the Requirements of the Department of the Army,* the call signal for opening of the draw as given by a United States Government vessel is _____ blast(s) of a whistle, horn or megaphone or _____ strokes of a bell.

    A. one; one
    B. two; two
    C. three; three
    D. four; four

15. With reference to a two-leaf, bascule bridge, a cover plate to minimize the open distance of the break of the leaves is known as the

    A. end dam
    B. center dam
    C. end fascia
    D. center fascia

16. A knot which forms a non-slipping loop is GENERALLY called a

    A. timber hitch
    B. half hitch
    C. square knot
    D. bowline knot

17. As a personal safety precaution, portable electric tools should be

    A. grounded
    B. used with a strong and lasting two-wire cord
    C. properly fused
    D. provided with an unbreakable two-way connector

18. A combination of steel members, such as beams, bars, ties, or the like, usually arranged in a triangle or collections of triangles so as to form a rigid framework and used in bridges, is USUALLY called a bridge

    A. gusset
    B. stringer
    C. truss
    D. trunnion

19. If an electric motor is overlubricated regularly, the statement MOST NEARLY CORRECT is that the

    A. motor life will be increased
    B. motor operating temperature will decrease
    C. result may be an oil soaked motor insulation
    D. oil ring may not operate properly due to lack of friction

20. If an assistant bridge operator earns $24,500 in the first six months of a year, and receives a 10% raise in salary for the next six months of the same year, his total earnings for the year will be MOST NEARLY

    A. $50,900
    B. $51,450
    C. $52,750
    D. $53,950

21. Spontaneous combustion is USUALLY caused by the combination of poor ventilation and

    A. oily waste
    B. half-filled paint cans
    C. exposed oil cans
    D. exposed grease cans

22. Assume that an assistant bridge operator, while replacing an electric lightbulb, falls from a ladder. He is lying on the floor unconscious and appears to be in a serious condition. The MOST significant first aid rule to observe in this case is

    A. to give the injured man a drink of water
    B. to place the injured man on a cot and keep him warm
    C. to apply artificial respiration immediately
    D. not to move the injured man unless a doctor so orders

23. Section 203.160, Harlem River Bridges, states that the draw of the bridges which leave a clear space, between the undersides thereof and the high water of spring tides of 24 feet, shall not be opened for commercial or pleasure vessels at any other time than between

    A. 8:00 A.M. and 4:00 P.M.
    B. 8:00 A.M. and 5:00 P.M.
    C. 10:00 A.M. and 5:00 P.M.
    D. 10:00 A.M. and 4:00 P.M.

24. The valve that allows a liquid to flow in one direction only is GENERALLY known as a _____ valve.

    A. stop   B. gate   C. globe   D. check

25. A GOOD lubricant should always possess

    A. high viscosity
    B. animal oils
    C. minimum impurities
    D. mineral oils

26. In general, light-bodied oil lubricants are MOST suitable for

    A. chain drives and roller bearings
    B. light loads at high speeds
    C. heavy bearing pressures
    D. heavy loads at high speeds

27. A knot which may safely be used to join together two ropes of the same size but which is NOT safe for ropes of different sizes is the _____ knot.

    A. thief's   B. square   C. granny   D. crown

28. Of the following, the one that is known as a type of roadway gate is the _____ gate.

    A. relief   B. valve   C. semantics   D. semaphore

29. In reference to a bridge, the dead load is USUALLY understood as the

    A. total weight of the moving cars
    B. extra weight carried by the trucks
    C. weight of the foundation
    D. weight of the structure

30. Slack in cables and tie rods is USUALLY taken up by using a(n)

    A. stillson wrench
    B. adjustable anchor bolt
    C. toggle bolt
    D. turnbuckle

31. When temperature changes from cold to warm, iron pipes, steel cable, and structural steel will USUALLY

   A. contract
   B. crystallize
   C. expand
   D. shear

32. Assume that the following information is a record of dates when certain tugs pass the draw of any bridges:
   Tug #1: June 30, July 1 to 9 inclusive, August 1 to 7 inclusive
   Tug #2: June 1 to 5 inclusive, June 16 to 20 inclusive
   Tug #3: June 2 to June 11 inclusive
   Tug #4: June 23 to July 3 inclusive
   According to *Regulations to Govern the Opening of Drawbridges Across the River* and the information given above, the one of the following groups of tugs which contain all of the tugs *habitually* using the draw is

   A. #3 and #4
   B. #1, #2, and #4
   C. #1, #3, and #4
   D. #2 and #3

33. A good disinfectant for a slightly cut finger is

   A. methyl alcohol
   B. carron oil
   C. mercurochrome
   D. resorcinol

34. If you think the rules and regulations of the department are unwise,

   A. disregard them and use your own judgment
   B. carry them out regardless of your opinion
   C. do nothing until some changes are made
   D. make the necessary changes and carry them out

35. Some of the men in the bridge crew have the faculty of knowing when there is work to be done and do not have to be prodded into doing it. These men may be said to possess

   A. initiative
   B. individuality
   C. obedience
   D. perseverance

KEY (CORRECT ANSWERS)

1. D
2. D
3. C
4. C
5. D

6. B
7. D
8. A
9. C
10. B

11. C
12. D
13. A
14. D
15. B

16. D
17. A
18. C
19. C
20. B

21. A
22. D
23. C
24. D
25. C

26. B
27. B
28. D
29. D
30. D

31. C
32. D
33. C
34. B
35. A

TEST 3

DIRECTIONS: Each question or incomplete statement is followed by several suggested answers or completions. Select the one that BEST answers the question or completes the statement. *PRINT THE LETTER OF THE CORRECT ANSWER IN THE SPACE AT THE RIGHT.*

1. To prevent nuts on the bolts holding down equipment from loosening due to vibration, it is BEST to use 1.____

    A. expansion shields
    B. lock washers
    C. lead washers
    D. brass washers

2. Flux is used in soldering PRINCIPALLY to 2.____

    A. roughen the surfaces
    B. retain the heat
    C. keep the surfaces clean
    D. lubricate the surfaces

3. In loosening a nut, a socket wrench with a ratchet would be used in preference to other types of wrenches if 3.____

    A. the nut is out of reach
    B. the turning space for the handle is limited
    C. much leverage is required
    D. the nut is worn

4. If a hammer head is loose on the wooden handle, the PROPER way to correct this defect is to 4.____

    A. drive a thicker wedge into the head end of the handle
    B. drive a nail into the head end of the handle
    C. soak the hammer in water
    D. drive the handle further into the head

5. An IMPORTANT difference between a fine file and a coarse file is that the fine file has 5.____

    A. mainly curved cuts
    B. deeper cuts
    C. less cuts per inch
    D. more cuts per inch

6. A stillson wrench should NOT be used on a hexagonal nut because the 6.____

    A. threads of the nut will be stripped
    B. flats of the nut may be damaged
    C. nut cannot be fully tightened
    D. stillson wrench is too difficult to adjust

7. For PROPER hand filing, the cut should be on 7.____

    A. both the forward and the return pass of the file with a steady stroke
    B. both the forward and the return pass of the file with a rocking motion
    C. the return pass of the file
    D. the forward pass of the file

8. The BEST type of knot for tieing together the ends of two ropes of the same size securely and without jamming is a

   A. granny knot
   B. square knot
   C. sheep shank
   D. half hitch

9. A hacksaw blade with 32 teeth per inch is BEST used to cut

   A. 2" diameter mild steel bar
   B. large sections of tough steel
   C. angle iron or heavy pipe
   D. thin wall tubing

10. A hacksaw blade with 14 teeth per inch is BEST used to cut

    A. large sections of mild steel
    B. large sections of tough steel
    C. angle iron
    D. large sections of brass or copper

11. The fraction which is equal to .375 is

    A. 3/16   B. 3/8   C. 5/8   D. 3/4

12. The sum of 3 1/8, 4 1/4, 4 5/8 is

    A. 12   B. 11 7/8   C. 11 3/4   D. 11 5/8

13. If a piece of wood 1'3 1/2" is put from a board 8'2" long, the length of the remaining board is MOST NEARLY

    A. 6'7 1/2"   B. 6'9 1/2"   C. 6'10 1/2"   D. 7'1 1/2"

14. One gallon of a certain paint can cover an area of 400 square feet with one coat of paint. Your superior tells you to paint an area 30 feet by 80 feet with this paint. The amount of paint required, in gallons, is MOST NEARLY

    A. 5   B. 6   C. 7   D. 8

15. When cleaning floors contaminated with oil and grease, it is BEST to use water and a good

    A. abrasive   B. detergent   C. deodorant   D. bleach

16. One-quarter divided by five-eighths is

    A. 5/32   B. 1/10   C. 2/5   D. 5/2

17. To prevent the electrolyte in the storage battery of an auxiliary gasoline engine from freezing, it is BEST to

    A. keep the battery fully charged
    B. add alcohol to the electrolyte
    C. add prestone to the electrolyte
    D. add distilled water to the electrolyte during the cold season

18. Of the following knots, the one which it is BEST to use to secure a rope to a piece of timber in order to haul it is a

    A. pole knot
    B. bowline
    C. timber hitch
    D. boat knot

19. A man works on a certain job continuously, with no time off for lunch. If he works from 9:45 A.M. until 1:35 P.M. to finish the job, the total time which he spent on the job is MOST NEARLY _____ hours, _____ minutes.

    A. 3; 10   B. 3; 35   C. 3; 50   D. 4; 15

20. A rectangular storage room is 15 feet by 16 feet, and the ceiling height is 10 feet. The volume of this room, in cubic feet, is MOST NEARLY

    A. 2,200   B. 2,300   C. 2,400   D. 2,500

21. One-quarter of the 168 lightbulbs on a certain bridge are replaced during the year. If these bulbs cost the city 21 cents each, the yearly cost of replacing the bulbs is MOST NEARLY

    A. $8.40   B. $8.82   C. $8.86   D. $8.92

22. If 14,229 is divided by 17, the result is MOST NEARLY

    A. 737   B. 747   C. 837   D. 847

23. A worker receives $17.15 per hour. In 15 working hours, his total earnings should be

    A. $256.05   B. $256.25   C. $257.05   D. $257.25

24. Previous to painting an existing iron railing that has been weathered, it is BEST to

    A. wash it with kerosene
    B. wipe it clean with a rag
    C. chip and scrape it free from rust
    D. wash it down with a good detergent

25. In the summer time when the temperature is extremely high, it is sometimes necessary to wet down the bridge. The BEST method to do this is to

    A. swab the bridge with a mop
    B. use a manual sprinkling bucket
    C. use a hose attached to a water line
    D. douse only the vital parts of the bridge structure with a pail of water

26. The one of the following substances which is commonly used on roadways for melting ice is

    A. potash
    B. maltose
    C. rock salt
    D. Rochelle salt

27. An assistant bridge operator should be attentive. As used in this sentence, the word attentive means MOST NEARLY

    A. watchful   B. prompt   C. negligent   D. willing

28. The assistant bridge operator reported a cavity in the roadway. As used in this sentence, cavity means MOST NEARLY

    A. lump B. wreck C. hollow D. oil-slick

29. Anyone working in traffic must be cautious. As used in this sentence, cautious means MOST NEARLY

    A. brave B. careful C. expert D. fast

30. The bridge operator refused to alter the original orders which he had issued to the assistant bridge operators.
    As used in this sentence, alter means MOST NEARLY

    A. toughen B. explain C. cancel D. change

31. The man who committed the error was very sheepish when questioned. As used in this sentence, sheepish means MOST NEARLY

    A. embarrassed B. offensive
    C. calm D. secretive

32. The bridge operator stated that the man responsible for the accident had auburn hair. As used in this sentence, the word auburn means MOST NEARLY

    A. reddish-brown B. signed
    C. thin D. silver-grey

33. The old man could do only routine work. As used in this sentence, routine means MOST NEARLY

    A. varied B. customary C. delivery D. light

34. The current in an electrical circuit can be calculated by dividing the voltage by the resistance in ohms. In a certain circuit, the resistance is 30 ohms and the voltage is 120 volts. The current in the circuit is _____ ampere(s).

    A. 1/4 B. 4 C. 30 D. 40

35. The freezing point of fresh water at sea level is MOST NEARLY

    A. 42° F B. 32° F C. 22° F D. 0° F

KEY (CORRECT ANSWERS)

1.	B	16.	C
2.	C	17.	A
3.	B	18.	C
4.	A	19.	C
5.	D	20.	C
6.	B	21.	B
7.	D	22.	C
8.	B	23.	D
9.	D	24.	C
10.	A	25.	C
11.	B	26.	C
12.	A	27.	A
13.	C	28.	C
14.	B	29.	B
15.	C	30.	D

31. A
32. A
33. B
34. B
35. B

EXAMINATION SECTION
TEST 1

DIRECTIONS: Each question or incomplete statement is followed by several suggested answers or completions. Select the one that BEST answers the question or completes the statement. *PRINT THE LETTER OF THE CORRECT ANSWER IN THE SPACE AT THE RIGHT.*

1. When the term *1/4-20* is used in connection with machine screws, the number 20 refers to the

    A. number of threads per inch
    B. length of the screw
    C. thickness of the screw
    D. diameter of the hole

    1.___

2. To take up slack in cables and tie rods, the proper device to use is USUALLY a

    A. clamp
    B. turnbuckle
    C. drift pin
    D. set screw

    2.___

3. The PRINCIPAL reason for *whipping* or *seizing* the end of a piece of rope is to

    A. make it more flexible
    B. reduce its diameter
    C. prevent the strands from unraveling
    D. prevent the end from rotting

    3.___

4. In order to properly and safely use a wrench with an adjustable jaw, the wrench should be so placed that the

    A. stationary jaw will be located forward in the direction in which the handle is to be turned
    B. movable jaw will be located forward in the direction in which the handle is to be turned
    C. jaws are perpendicular to the plane on which the handle is to be turned and above the work
    D. jaws are perpendicular to the plane in which the handle is to be turned and below the work

    4.___

5. For manually lifting a heavy object, which is flat on the floor, in order to place rollers under it, it is BEST to use a

    A. bumper jack
    B. 2x4 stud
    C. crowbar
    D. long iron pipe

    5.___

6. The PROPER time to clean tools, in order to be sure that they stay in good condition, is

    A. as soon after using them as possible
    B. just before using them
    C. whenever they are dirty enough to be unsafe
    D. whenever work is slack

    6.___

7. Of the following methods of storing rope, the one which is the BEST and SAFEST is:

   A. Hang the rope in loose coils in a dry, well-ventilated place
   B. Hang the rope in loose coils in a humid, tightly closed room
   C. Lay the rope on the floor of a humid but well-ventilated room
   D. Lay the rope on a lime-covered floor in a dry well-ventilated room

8. If it is difficult to loosen a nut with a certain open end wrench, the SAFEST and BEST procedure is to

   A. strike the handle of the wrench with a sledge until the nut is loosened
   B. use a piece of pipe to increase the leverage on the wrench
   C. oil the jaws of the wrench
   D. use another wrench having a sufficiently long handle

9. For safe operation of a portable electric drill, the metal frame of the drill should be

   A. painted with waterproof paint
   B. painted red
   C. buffed to a high polish
   D. grounded

10. When a portable ladder 24 feet long is placed against a wall but is NOT held by a man or fastened in any way, the MAXIMUM safe horizontal distance between the foot of the ladder and the wall is _____ feet.

    A. 12   B. 9   C. 6   D. 3

11. Artificial respiration should be started immediately on a man who has suffered electric shock if he is

    A. unconscious and breathing
    B. conscious and in a daze
    C. unconscious and not breathing
    D. conscious and badly burned

12. One good safety rule is that an electric hand tool, such as a drill, should never be lifted or carried by its service cord. The PRIMARY reason for this rule is that the

    A. cord might pull off its terminal and become short-circuited
    B. tool might swing and be damaged by striking some hard object
    C. rubber covering of the cord might overstretch
    D. tool may slip out of the hand as it is hard to get a good grip on a slick rubber cord

13. If a fuse of higher rating than the current rating is used in an electrical circuit,

    A. serious damage may result to the circuit from overload
    B. better protection will be obtained
    C. the fuse will blow more often since it carries more current
    D. maintenance of the larger fuses will be higher

14.

The force F required to lift the 30# weight is the GREATEST in the case of the lever used in the figure above designated by
A. 1   B. 2   C. 3   D. 4

Questions 15-17.

DIRECTIONS: Questions 15 through 17, inclusive, are to be answered in accordance with the information given in the following paragraph.

Tides are the periodic rise and fall of ocean waters, occurring about twice a day, becoming later each day, ...due to the gravitational pull of the moon and to a smaller extent the sun.... The tides rise highest when the sun and moon are on the same side of the earth (Spring tides) and lowest (neap tides) when the sun and moon are in opposition. Local tides depend on irregularities in the floor and coast of the ocean.

15. According to the above paragraph, if high tide is at 7 A.M. on a certain day, the next day's high tide FIRST occurs

   A. slightly earlier than 7 A.M.
   B. slightly later than 7 A.M.
   C. at exactly 7 A.M.
   D. at exactly 7 P.M.

16. According to the above paragraph, the HIGHEST tides are called _____ tides.

   A. spring   B. summer   C. fall   D. winter

17. According to the above paragraph, the neap tides occur when the

   A. moon is in its third quarter
   B. moon and sun are on the same side of the earth
   C. sun and moon are in opposition
   D. moon is in its first quarter

18. Water should NOT be used to extinguish fires in or around electrical apparatus. The MAIN reason for this is that water

   A. may cause the circuit fuses to blow
   B. may conduct electric current and cause a shock hazard
   C. will corrode the electrical conductors
   D. will damage the insulation

19. The BEST way to ensure safety on the job is to

    A. be alert
    B. check every move with your supervisor
    C. work very slowly
    D. follow every rule

20. The instrument which is used to check the charge of a storage battery is a

    A. hydrometer   B. hygrometer
    C. thermometer   D. wattmeter

21. The tip of a soldering iron is made of copper because

    A. copper is a very good conductor of heat
    B. solder will not stick to other metals
    C. copper is the cheapest metal available
    D. the melting point of copper is higher than that of iron

Questions 22-35.

DIRECTIONS: Questions 22 through 35, inclusive, are to be answered in accordance with the information given in the paragraph below.

At 8:30 A.M. on Friday, February 2, 2009, assistant bridge operator Henry Jones started to clean the walk of the Avenue X Bridge. It was snowing heavily and the surface of the road was slippery. At 8:32 A.M., Mr. Jones saw a westbound station wagon skid and strike a westbound sedan about 50 feet from the barrier. Both cars were badly damaged. The station wagon was overturned and came to rest 8 feet from the barrier. The woman driver of the station wagon, Mrs. Harriet White, was thrown clear and landed in the middle of the road. The other car was smashed against the barrier. The driver of the sedan, Mr. Tom Green, was pinned behind the steering wheel, and suffered cuts about the face. Mr. Jones called the bridge operator, Mr. Frank Smith, who telephoned for an ambulance. First aid was given to both drivers. They were taken to the Avenue W Hospital by an ambulance which was driven by Mr. James Doe and arrived on the scene at 9:07 A.M. Patrolman John Brown, Badge No. 71162, had arrived before the ambulance and recorded all the details of the accident, including the statements of Mr. Henry Jones and of Mr. Jack Black, another eyewitness.

22. The accident occurred on

    A. Saturday, February 3, 2008
    B. Friday, February 2, 2008
    C. Friday, February 2, 2009
    D. Friday, February 3, 2009

23. The time of the accident was

    A. 7:32 A.M.   B. 8:32 A.M.   C. 8:32 P.M.   D. 7:32 P.M.

24. The assistant bridge operator's name was

    A. Frank Smith   B. Tom Jones
    C. Henry Smith   D. Henry Jones

25. The accident involved a

    A. sedan and a station wagon
    B. station wagon and a panel truck
    C. station wagon and two sedans
    D. sedan and two station wagons

26. The man named Jack Black was a(n)

    A. patrolman   B. eyewitness
    C. ambulance driver   D. street cleaner

27. The time which elapsed between the accident and the arrival of the ambulance was MOST NEARLY _____ minutes.

    A. 7   B. 28   C. 32   D. 35

28. The weather was

    A. fair   B. rainy   C. sleety   D. snowy

29. The station wagon was driven by

    A. Jane Brown   B. Jane White
    C. Harriet White   D. Harriet Brown

30. Tom Green was the

    A. driver of the ambulance   B. driver of the sedan
    C. other eyewitness   D. patrolman

31. The barrier was

    A. struck by the sedan
    B. struck by the station wagon
    C. struck by both cars
    D. not struck by either car

32. The damage done to

    A. both cars was slight
    B. the sedan was severe but that done to the station wagon was slight
    C. the station wagon was severe but that done to the sedan was slight
    D. both cars was severe

33. The woman driver

    A. was pinned behind the wheel
    B. suffered face cuts
    C. was thrown clear
    D. was trapped in the car

34. The name of the bridge operator was

    A. Frank Smith   B. John Smith
    C. Henry Jones   D. Frank Jones

35. When the accident occurred, the _____ from the barrier.

    A. station wagon was 20 ft.
    B. cars were 50 ft.
    C. sedan was 60 ft.
    D. sedan was 8 ft.

35._____

KEY (CORRECT ANSWERS)

1. A	16. A
2. B	17. B
3. C	18. B
4. B	19. A
5. C	20. A
6. A	21. A
7. A	22. C
8. D	23. B
9. D	24. D
10. C	25. A
11. C	26. B
12. A	27. D
13. A	28. D
14. B	29. C
15. C	30. B

31. A
32. D
33. C
34. A
35. B

TEST 2

DIRECTIONS: Each question or incomplete statement is followed by several suggested answers or completions. Select the one that BEST answers the question or completes the statement. *PRINT THE LETTER OF THE CORRECT ANSWER IN THE SPACE AT THE RIGHT.*

1. The responsibility for the operation of many movable bridges belongs to the   1.___

    A. Department of Public Works
    B. Department of Marine and Aviation
    C. Department of Traffic
    D. police department

2. Of the following types of bridges, the one that is NOT a movable bridge is a   2.___

    A. draw   B. suspension   C. lift   D. bascule

3. Some bridges are not opened during hours of the day when there is very heavy auto traffic. The PRINCIPAL reason for this is to   3.___

    A. reduce possibilities of accidents
    B. speed up operation of the bridge
    C. reduce cost of operation
    D. prevent long traffic tie-ups

4. The driver of an auto has been injured in an accident on a lift bridge. The FIRST thing that should be done is   4.___

    A. move the car so the bridge can be opened
    B. stop all traffic from crossing the bridge
    C. put out warning lights so boats know the bridge cannot be opened
    D. call an ambulance

5. During working hours you cut your finger slightly. The FIRST thing you should do is   5.___

    A. call a doctor
    B. wash your finger with soap and water
    C. call the main office and ask to be relieved
    D. make out an accident report

6. An electric motor should never be cleaned while it is running. The PRINCIPAL reason for this is that   6.___

    A. it is impossible to clean a running motor properly
    B. the motor may be damaged if the cleaning rag is accidentally dropped
    C. the person cleaning the motor may be injured
    D. it is quicker and easier to clean a motor when it is not running

7. When oil spills on a floor, the FIRST thing to do is to   7.___

    A. wash the floor with soap and water
    B. soak the oil up with sawdust

35

C. sweep the oil with a fiber brush
D. wipe up with a rag soaked in gasoline

8. One of the CHIEF causes of accidents in mechanical work is

   A. working slowly
   B. using more care than is necessary
   C. using the wrong tool for the job
   D. two men doing the work of one

9. The BEST method of determining which of a group of fuses is burnt out is with a

   A. light tester   B. tachometer
   C. hydrometer   D. induction coil

10. For safe bridge operation, it is IMPORTANT that the operators should always

    A. observe the rules and regulations
    B. come to work on time
    C. keep themselves occupied
    D. be courteous

11. Water is NOT used in cleaning electric panel boards because water

    A. is not an effective cleaner
    B. will rust the copper bus-bars
    C. is not always available in the power station
    D. will conduct electricity

12. If a worker must repair an electric circuit that is live, he should wear

    A. safety goggles   B. rubber gloves
    C. a hard hat   D. coveralls

13. A piece of equipment used to raise or lower the voltage of an electric circuit is a

    A. transformer   B. resistor
    C. wattmeter   D. condenser

14. For safe operation, the part of an electric motor that should be grounded is the

    A. frame   B. armature   C. brushes   D. field

15. When an electrical fuse blows, it is BEST to

    A. replace it with the fuse of the next larger rating
    B. open the main circuit breaker
    C. put a piece of copper between the fuse terminals
    D. replace it with a fuse of the same rating

16. If a circuit breaker opens and when closed it opens again, it is BEST to

    A. replace it with a breaker of a larger capacity
    B. replace it with a fuse
    C. replace it with a breaker of a smaller capacity
    D. have the circuit checked

17. Steel steps are frequently coated with an abrasive. The PRINCIPAL reason for this coating is to

    A. reduce cost of maintenance
    B. prevent slipping
    C. improve the appearance
    D. make it easier to paint

18. A 20-ft. ladder is placed against a vertical wall as shown in the sketch at the right.
    Of the following values for the distance D, shown in the sketch, the one which is SAFEST is _____ ft.

    A. 1
    B. 5
    C. 9
    D. 12

19. Storing of oily waste and rags presents a safety hazard because under certain conditions they may EASILY

    A. begin to burn
    B. fall apart when used
    C. become very stiff
    D. become too wet and soggy

20. *The foreman is the keyman in safety in any working group.* As used in this sentence, keyman means MOST NEARLY

    A. watchman
    B. most important man
    C. man to whom to bring problems
    D. man who issues safety tools

21. *It is best to find small defects before they can do great damage.* As used in this sentence, defects means MOST NEARLY

    A. faults   B. shorts   C. bearings   D. dangers

22. *It is easier and cheaper to maintain equipment than to repair the equipment when it is too late.* As used in this sentence, maintain means MOST NEARLY

    A. buy good
    B. use up
    C. keep in good condition
    D. throw away

Questions 23-25.

DIRECTIONS: Questions 23 through 25, inclusive, are to be answered in accordance with the paragraphs below.

The proper use of artificial respiration is of the greatest importance when breathing has stopped in cases of electric shock, gas poisoning or drowning.

The first minutes in applying artificial respiration are most important. It should start immediately and be continued without interruption (if necessary for four hours) until natural breathing is restored. Someone else should call the doctor.

The first step in cases of electric shock is to instantly break the contact. Any available non-conductor can be used for this purpose, but the hands of the individual applying artificial respiration must be protected to avoid further accident (if possible, shut off the current or break the circuit).

The victim of gas poisoning must immediately receive fresh air, preferably in a warm dry atmosphere. Use proper protective equipment before entering gas-filled atmosphere. If such equipment is not available, hold your breath while you dash in and drag out the victim.

23. In cases of electric shock, the FIRST step to take is to

    A. lay the victim face down and start artificial respiration
    B. give the victim a stimulant
    C. break the contact with the live circuit
    D. put a blanket over the victim

24. In cases of gas poisoning, the FIRST step to take is to

    A. lay the victim face down and take foreign objects out of his mouth
    B. give the victim a stimulant
    C. cover the victim with blankets
    D. take the victim out of the gas-filled atmosphere and into the fresh air

25. Artificial respiration should be continued

    A. for half an hour only
    B. for two or three hours only
    C. until the victim's face becomes flushed
    D. until the victim's natural breathing is restored or a physician tells you to stop

Questions 26-29.

DIRECTIONS: Questions 26 through 29, inclusive, are to be answered in accordance with the paragraphs below.

Lay the victim face down, with one arm extended directly overhead, the other arm bent at the elbow with his face turned outward resting on hand or forearm to keep nose and mouth free for breathing. Kneel straddling the victim's hips with the knees just below the patient's hip bones. Place your palms on the small of his back, with fingers on ribs, little finger just touching the lowest rib. This is important as placing fingers too high may cause a rib injury; placing them too low puts pressure on kidneys where it does no good and may do harm.

Swing forward gradually bringing your weight to bear. Keep arms stiff. Shoulders should be directly over back of hand. After about two seconds, release pressure gradually by swinging back on your heels and letting hands drop. Repeat this sequence of operations smoothly and rhythmically.

While you continue artificial respiration, any helpers you may have should take any foreign objects (if any) out of the victim's mouth, cover him with blankets or coats, and send for a doctor immediately.

26. In applying artificial respiration, you should kneel straddling the victim with your knees

    A. just below the shoulders
    B. halfway between the small of the back and the shoulders
    C. midway between the mid-point of the thighs and the knees
    D. just below the hip-bones

27. One of the MOST important reasons why the hands should not be placed too low in applying artificial respiration is that this

    A. may result in a broken rib
    B. may injure the liver
    C. does no good
    D. is likely to cause the victim to inhale when he should exhale

28. In applying artificial respiration, you should swing forward

    A. quickly with arms stiff
    B. quickly with arms bent
    C. gradually with arms bent
    D. gradually with arms stiff

29. While you are giving artificial respiration, your assistants should

    A. give the victim a stimulant and cover him with blankets immediately
    B. take foreign objects out of the victim's mouth and give him a stimulant immediately
    C. dash water in his face and give him a drink of water immediately
    D. take foreign objects out of his mouth and send for a doctor immediately

30. An eye is to be formed in a rope. The metal ring used to line this eye is called a

    A. thimble   B. swedge   C. rosette   D. hickey

31. In order to fasten a piece of machinery to a concrete floor, several holes must be made in the concrete. The BEST tool to use for this work is a

    A. round nose chisel   B. twist drill
    C. star drill   D. diamond point chisel

Questions 32-33.

DIRECTIONS: Questions 32 and 33, respectively, refer to the figures in the sketch below.

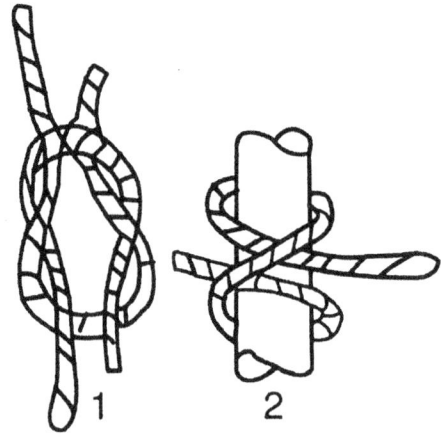

32. The rope knot shown in Figure 1 above is a

    A. bowline
    B. timber hitch
    C. sheep shank
    D. square knot

33. The rope knot shown in Figure 2 above is a

    A. square knot
    B. timber hitch
    C. sheep shank
    D. clove hitch

34. The total automobile traffic of a bridge increased from 33,000 to 37,000. This represents an increase of APPROXIMATELY

    A. 8% B. 12% C. 16% D. 20%

35. Eighty percent of the vessels passing under a certain bridge are tugboats. If 105 vessels pass under this bridge daily, the number of tugboats passing under the bridge daily is MOST NEARLY

    A. 80 B. 84 C. 88 D. 92

36. A certain shelf can safely hold 140 pounds. On the shelf is a 45 lb. carton of nuts and bolts, a 52 lb. carton of assorted hardware, and two containers of lead paint weighing 27 lbs. each. The shelf

    A. is overloaded by 16 lbs.
    B. can safely hold an additional 16 lbs.
    C. is overloaded by 11 lbs.
    D. can safely hold an additional 11 lbs.

37. Of the following decimals, the one which has the same value as 3/8 is

    A. 0.125 B. 0.266 C. 0.333 D. 0.375

38. If an iron bar 6'6 1/8" long is cut in half, the length of each piece will then be MOST NEARLY 3'

    A. 3 1/16"   B. 3 1/8"   C. 6 1/8"   D. 6 1/4"

39. The amount of liquid that can be stored in 72 one-quart cans is _____ gallons.

    A. 9   B. 18   C. 24   D. 36

40. Salt is frequently put on any icy pavement. The PRINCIPAL reason for this is that salt

    A. is an abrasive and will prevent skidding
    B. will tend to melt the ice
    C. will reduce the glare from the ice
    D. will reflect the headlights from cars at night

KEY (CORRECT ANSWERS)

1. A	11. D	21. A	31. C
2. B	12. B	22. C	32. D
3. D	13. A	23. C	33. D
4. D	14. A	24. D	34. B
5. B	15. D	25. D	35. B
6. C	16. D	26. D	36. C
7. C	17. B	27. C	37. D
8. B	18. B	28. D	38. A
9. A	19. A	29. D	39. B
10. A	20. B	30. A	40. B

TEST 3

DIRECTIONS: Each question or incomplete statement is followed by several suggested answers or completions. Select the one that BEST answers the question or completes the statement. *PRINT THE LETTER OF THE CORRECT ANSWER IN THE SPACE AT THE RIGHT.*

1. Penetrating oil is MOST commonly used when

   A. a lot of oil is necessary
   B. the part to be oiled is thick
   C. a rusted bolt is to be loosened
   D. a quick job must be done

   1.____

2. Screws are used in wood in preference to nails PRINCIPALLY because screws

   A. are cheaper
   B. are easier to drive
   C. are less likely to split the wood
   D. hold better

   2.____

3. The gauge number of wire refers to the wire

   A. diameter   B. weight   C. length   D. cost

   3.____

4. The liquid MOST frequently used to cool a chisel when it is being ground on a grindstone is

   A. turpentine   B. benzine
   C. carbon tetrachloride   D. water

   4.____

5. Of the following, the electrical device which is COMMONLY used to supply mechanical energy to run machinery is a(n)

   A. electric generator   B. electric motor
   C. storage battery   D. rectifier

   5.____

6. A bolt that has threads on both ends is called a

   A. carriage bolt   B. stud
   C. machine screw   D. lag screw

   6.____

7. The temperature at which water will become ice under normal conditions is MOST NEARLY

   A. 0° F   B. 32° F   C. 110° F   D. 212° F

   7.____

8. The type of saw MOST commonly used to cut a metal bar in two is a _____ saw.

   A. crosscut   B. buck   C. coping   D. hack

   8.____

9. The tool which can readily be used for holding or bending wire is a

   A. pair of pliers   B. wrench
   C. plumb bob   D. spoke shave

   9.____

10. The one of the following tools which is MOST generally used to tighten a pipe is a(n) 10.____

    A. monkey wrench B. Stillson wrench
    C. box wrench   D. pair of nippers

11. Lock washers are MOST commonly used with 11.____

    A. rivets   B. cotter pins
    C. machine screws D. wood screws

12. Some work which you have to do requires that you reach a point higher up on a vertical wall. You find that you cannot reach this point by using either one of two ladders you have with you. Of the following, the SAFEST and MOST CORRECT procedure is to 12.____

    A. set the longer of the two ladders on two large packing boxes set one on top of another
    B. splice the two ladders together
    C. set the longer ladder on a strong box and climb up until you stand on the top rung
    D. get another ladder of sufficient length to permit you to do the job

13. 13.____

    Wheel A turns in a clockwise direction. Wheel C will turn _____ than wheel A in a _____ direction.
    A. faster; clockwise   B. faster; counterclockwise
    C. slower; clockwise   D. slower; counterclockwise

14. A metal surface which is coated with rust is to be painted. Before this surface is painted, it should be 14.____

    A. coated with shellac
    B. washed with water
    C. scraped or chipped
    D. washed with a salt solution

15. To fasten a small metal cabinet to a hollow tile wall, it is BEST to use 15.____

    A. expansion bolts B. toggle bolts
    C. stove bolts   D. lag screws

16. A machine tap can be PROPERLY used to 16.____

    A. siphon fluid from a bucket
    B. thread a rod
    C. cut internal threads in a hole
    D. set a rivet

17. The one of the following types of wrenches which CANNOT be used to tighten a hex head bolt is a(n) _____ wrench.

    A. box
    B. monkey
    C. adjustable open end
    D. allen

Questions 18-22.

DIRECTIONS: Questions 18 through 22, inclusive, are to be answered in accordance with the paragraph below.

When reporting for work each day, an assistant bridge operator is required to sign his time card. At this time, he will read the notices published on the bulletin board for any changes in rules or special conditions that may affect him. After changing into work clothes, the supervisor will assign the assistant bridge operator to any work that has to be done. When the bridge is not open, there may be tasks such as cleaning the motor room, oiling the machinery or minor repair work. When the bridge is to be opened, the assistant bridge operator will go to his post at one end of the bridge and will signal all traffic to stop by means of lights. Immediately thereafter, he will start to lower the barricades. However, the barricades will not be completely lowered until all traffic has stopped. The bridge is then opened.

18. According to the above paragraph, the FIRST thing an assistant bridge operator does when reporting for work is to

    A. read the bulletin board
    B. change to work clothes
    C. sign his time card
    D. report to his supervisor

19. The purpose of reading the bulletin board is to

    A. find out what work has to be done
    B. see who the supervisor is
    C. save time
    D. be aware of any changes in rules

20. Work to which the assistant bridge operator may be assigned is

    A. oiling the motors
    B. hand signaling traffic
    C. replacing the lift cables
    D. opening the bridge

21. Lowering of the barricades is begun

    A. before signaling the traffic to stop
    B. at the same time as the traffic is signaled to stop
    C. immediately after the traffic is signaled to stop
    D. after all traffic has stopped

22. The drawbridge is opened when

    A. starting to lower the barricades
    B. signaling traffic to stop
    C. the barricades are completely lowered
    D. it appears all traffic has stopped

23. If a supervisor gives you a job that you do not know how to do, you should

    A. do the job as well as you can
    B. ask a fellow worker how to do the job
    C. tell the supervisor to get someone else to do the job
    D. ask the supervisor for instructions on how to do the job

24. If you feel that you are always getting the *dirty* assignments on a job, you should

    A. keep quiet and do the work anyway
    B. slow down your work so that your supervisor will realize you are dissatisfied
    C. take your feelings out on the other employees
    D. talk the matter over with your supervisor

25. An approaching vessel signals the bridge for the opening of the draw. This vessel has its smoke stack located astern and displays a vivid red flag. From this description, it can only be properly said that this vessel is a(n)

    A. sea-going passenger ship   B. aircraft carrier
    C. oil tanker   D. R.R. barge

Questions 26-34.

DIRECTIONS: Questions 26 through 34, inclusive, are to be answered in accordance with the rules listed below.

RULES FOR BRIDGE OPERATION

When a vessel owned by the United States Government or the city approaches a movable bridge, it shall signal with four distinct blasts of a whistle.

All other vessels signal with three distinct blasts of a whistle.

All call signals for openings shall be answered promptly by the bridge by 2 long distinct blasts.

This signal indicates to the boat that the call signal has been heard and preparations to open will be made.

After this signal, the bridge operator shall open his bridge at such a time which in his judgment and experience will permit prompt passage of the boat without unreasonable delay and will not create any unreasonable delay to land traffic.

At no time shall the draw be moved until all sidewalk and roadway traffic gates are locked in their closed position.

If the draw cannot be opened, the 2 blast signal shall be repeated until acknowledged by the boat.

It is extremely important that the draw be brought to its fully opened position at all times, irrespective of the size of the boat. (This does not apply to test openings.)

When the draw is fully opened, the bridge operator shall sound the same signal as the call signal.

While the draw is in its fully opened position, no attempt shall be made toward closing until the passing boat has cleared the draw.

Except in rare emergencies, the draw shall not be moved either in closing or opening while there is a boat in the draw.

When the draw is fully closed and land traffic can be resumed, the bridge operator is to sound one blast which will be the signal for the bridge tenders to open all traffic gates.

Visual signals shall be used as prescribed by the Department of the Army whenever sound signals cannot be given or if sound signals cannot be heard.

The time of an opening shall be the interval between the time the traffic gates are closed and the time they are opened.

26. As used above, prompt means MOST NEARLY 26.____

    A. easy   B. safe   C. speedy   D. careful

27. As used above, extremely means MOST NEARLY 27.____

    A. very   B. mildly   C. of course   D. sometimes

28. As used above, visual means MOST NEARLY 28.____

    A. telegraph   B. bell   C. runner   D. sight

29. According to the above statements, if an approaching vessel signals for an opening with 4 blasts, it means that the vessel is 29.____

    A. a tanker
    B. a tug
    C. foreign-owned
    D. city-owned

30. According to the above rules, a boat approaching a bridge will signal the bridge by 30.____

    A. swinging a red light
    B. calling through a megaphone
    C. blowing a whistle
    D. waving a blue flag

31. According to the above rules, the bridge answers the boat by blowing a whistle 31.____

    A. once
    B. twice
    C. three times
    D. four times

32. According to the above rules, when a bridge is opened for passage of a boat, the amount that the bridge is opened will 32.____

    A. vary depending on the size of boat only
    B. vary depending on the tide only
    C. vary depending on the size of boat and the tide
    D. always be the same

33. According to the above rules, the operator normally will begin to close the bridge 33.____

    A. as soon as the boat enters the draw, so the operator knows the height of the boat
    B. when the center of the boat has passed the center of the bridge
    C. at any time convenient to the operator
    D. after the boat has completely passed through the draw

34. According to the above rules, the man operating the traffic gate knows the bridge is closed when he 34.____

    A. sees the bridge operator wave
    B. sees the traffic signals turn green
    C. feels the bridge come together
    D. hears a single blast on a whistle

35. Assume that a fellow worker is in contact with an electrically charged wire. Of the following, the BEST reason for NOT grasping the victim's clothing with your bare hands in order to pull him off the wire is that

    A. his clothing may be damp with perspiration
    B. his clothing may be 100% wool
    C. you may be standing on a dry surface
    D. you may be wearing leather-soled shoes

36. Suppose a man falls from a two-story-high scaffold and is unconscious. You should

    A. call for medical assistance and avoid moving the man
    B. get someone to help you move him indoors to a bed
    C. have someone help you walk him around until he revives
    D. hold his head up and pour a stimulant down his throat

37. For proper first aid treatment, a person who has fainted should be

    A. doused with cold water and then warmly covered
    B. given artificial respiration until he is revived
    C. laid down with his head lower than the rest of his body
    D. slapped on the face until he is revived

38. If you are called on to give first aid to a person who is suffering from shock, you should

    A. apply cold towels
    B. give him a stimulant
    C. keep him awake
    D. wrap him warmly

39. Artificial respiration would NOT be proper first aid for a person suffering from

    A. drowning
    B. electric shock
    C. external bleeding
    D. suffocation

40. Suppose you are called on to give first aid to several victims of an accident. First attention should be given to the one who is

    A. bleeding severely
    B. groaning loudly
    C. unconscious
    D. vomiting

KEY (CORRECT ANSWERS)

1. C	11. C	21. C	31. B
2. D	12. D	22. C	32. D
3. A	13. C	23. D	33. D
4. D	14. C	24. D	34. D
5. B	15. B	25. C	35. B
6. B	16. C	26. C	36. C
7. B	17. D	27. A	37. C
8. D	18. C	28. D	38. B
9. A	19. D	29. D	39. D
10. B	20. A	30. C	40. D

SAFETY
EXAMINATION SECTION
TEST 1

DIRECTIONS: Each question or incomplete statement is followed by several suggested answers or completions. Select the one that BEST answers the question or completes the statement. *PRINT THE LETTER OF THE CORRECT ANSWER IN THE SPACE AT THE RIGHT.*

1. Which one of the following is an INCORRECT safety guideline?   1.____

   A. All working conditions and equipment should be considered carefully before beginning an operation.
   B. Aisles should be lighted properly.
   C. Personnel should be provided with protective clothing essential to safe performance of a task.
   D. In manual lifting, the worker must keep his knees straight and lift with the arm muscles.

2. Of the following, the supply item with the GREATEST susceptibility to spontaneous heating is   2.____

   A. alcohol, ethyl   B. kerosene
   C. candles   D. turpentine

Questions 3-7.

DIRECTIONS: Questions 3 through 7 are descriptions of accidents that occurred in a warehouse. For each accident, choose the letter in front of the safety measure that is MOST likely to prevent a repetition of the accident indicated.

<u>SAFETY MEASURE</u>

   A. Posting warning signs
   B. Redesign of layout or facilities
   C. Repairing, improving or replacing supplies, tools or equipment
   D. Training the staff in safe practices

3. After a new all-glass door was installed at the entrance to the warehouse, one of the employees banged his head into the door causing a large lump on his forehead when he failed to realize that the door was closed.   3.____

4. While tieing up a package with manila rope, an employee got several small rope splinters in his right hand and he had to have medical treatment to remove the splinters.   4.____

5. An employee discovered a small fire in a wastepaper basket but was unable to prevent it from spreading because all the nearby fire extinguishers were inaccessible due to skids of material being stacked in front of the extinguishers.   5.____

6. When a laborer attempted to drop the tailgate of a delivery truck while the truck was being backed into the loading dock, he had his fingers crushed when the truck continued to move while he was working on lowering the tailgate.   6.____

7. An employee carrying a carton with both hands tripped over a broom which had been left lying in an aisle by another employee after the latter had swept the aisle. 7._____

8. Safety experts agree that accidents can probably BEST be prevented by 8._____

    A. developing safety consciousness among employees
    B. developing a program which publicizes major accidents
    C. penalizing employees the first time they do not follow safety procedures
    D. giving recognition to employees with accident-free records

9. The accident records of many agencies indicate that most on-the-job injuries are caused by the unsafe acts of their employees. 9._____
Which one of the following statements pinpoints the MOST probable cause of this safety problem?

    A. Responsibility for preventing on-the-job accidents has not been delegated.
    B. Lack of proper supervision has permitted these unsafe actions to continue.
    C. No consideration has been given to eliminating environmental job hazards.
    D. Penalties for causing on-the-job accidents are not sufficiently severe.

10. Which of the following methods is LEAST essential to the success of an accident prevention program? 10._____

    A. Determining corrective measures by analyzing the causes of accidents and making recommendations to eliminate them
    B. Educating employees as to the importance of safe working conditions and methods
    C. Determining accident causes by seeking out the conditions from which each accident has developed
    D. Holding each supervisor responsible for accidents occurring during the on-the-job performance of his immediate subordinates

11. The effectiveness of a public relations program in a public agency is BEST indicated by the 11._____

    A. amount of mass media publicity favorable to the policies of the agency
    B. morale of those employees who directly serve the patrons of the agency
    C. public's understanding and support of the agency's program and policies
    D. number of complaints received by the agency from patrons using its facilities

12. Buttered bread and coffee dropped on an office floor in a terminal are 12._____

    A. minor hazards which should cause no serious injury
    B. unattractive, but not dangerous
    C. the most dangerous types of office hazards
    D. hazards which should be corrected immediately

13. A laborer was sent upstairs to get a 20-pound sack of rock salt. While going downstairs and reading the printing on the sack, he fell, and the sack of rock salt fell and broke his toe. 13._____
Which of the following is MOST likely to have been the MOST important cause of the accident?
The

A. stairs were beginning to become worn
B. laborer was carrying too heavy a sack of rock salt
C. rock salt was in a place that was too inaccessible
D. laborer was not careful about the way he went down the stairs

14. A COMMONLY recommended safe distance between the foot of an extension ladder and the wall against which it is placed is

    A. 3 feet for ladders less than 18 feet in height
    B. between 3 feet and 6 feet for ladders less than 18 feet in length
    C. 1/8 the length of the extended ladder
    D. 1/4 the length of the extended ladder

15. The BEST type of fire extinguisher for electrical fires is the _____ extinguisher.

    A. dry chemical   B. foam
    C. carbon monoxide   D. baking soda-acid

16. A Class A extinguisher should be used for fires in

    A. potassium, magnesium, zinc, sodium
    B. electrical wiring
    C. oil, gasoline
    D. wood, paper, and textiles

17. The one of the following which is NOT a safe practice when lifting heavy objects is:

    A. Keep the back as nearly upright as possible
    B. If the object feels too heavy, keep lifting until you get help
    C. Spread the feet apart
    D. Use the arm and leg muscles

18. In a shop, it would be MOST necessary to provide a fitted cover on the metal container for

    A. old paint brushes   B. oily rags and waste
    C. sand   D. broken glass

19. Safety shoes usually have the unique feature of

    A. extra hard heels and soles to prevent nails from piercing the shoes
    B. special leather to prevent the piercing of the shoes by falling objects
    C. a metal guard over the toes which is built into the shoes
    D. a non-slip tread on the heels and soles

20. Of the following, the MOST important factor contributing to a helper's safety on the job is for him to

    A. work slowly   B. wear gloves
    C. be alert   D. know his job well

21. If it is necessary for you to lift one end of a piece of heavy equipment with a crowbar in order to allow a maintainer to work underneath it, the BEST of the following procedures to follow is to

    A. support the handle of the bar on a box
    B. insert temporary blocks to support the piece
    C. call the supervisor to help you
    D. wear heavy gloves

22. Of the following, the MOST important reason for not letting oily rags accumulate in an open storage bin is that they

    A. may start a fire by spontaneous combustion
    B. will drip oil onto other items in the bin
    C. may cause a foul odor
    D. will make the area messy

23. Of the following, the BEST method to employ in putting out a gasoline fire is to

    A. use a bucket of water
    B. smother it with rags
    C. use a carbon dioxide extinguisher
    D. use a carbon tetrachloride extinguisher

24. When opening an emergency exit door set in the sidewalk, the door should be raised slowly to avoid

    A. a sudden rush of air from the street
    B. making unnecessary noise
    C. damage to the sidewalk
    D. injuring pedestrians

25. The BEST reason to turn off lights when cleaning lampshades on electrical fixtures is to

    A. conserve energy
    B. avoid electrical shock
    C. prevent breakage of lightbulbs
    D. prevent unnecessary eye strain

KEY (CORRECT ANSWERS)

1. D
2. D
3. A
4. D
5. B

6. D
7. D
8. A
9. B
10. D

11. C
12. D
13. D
14. D
15. A

16. D
17. B
18. B
19. C
20. C

21. B
22. A
23. C
24. D
25. B

TEST 2

DIRECTIONS: Each question or incomplete statement is followed by several suggested answers or completions. Select the one that BEST answers the question or completes the statement. *PRINT THE LETTER OF THE CORRECT ANSWER IN THE SPACE AT THE RIGHT.*

1. The MOST important reason for roping off a work area in a terminal is to   1.____

    A. protect the public
    B. protect the repair crew
    C. prevent distraction of the crew by the public
    D. prevent delays to the public

2. Shoes which have a sponge rubber sole should NOT be worn around a work area because such a sole   2.____

    A. will wear quickly
    B. is not waterproof
    C. does not keep the feet warm
    D. is easily punctured by steel objects

3. When repair work is being done on an elevated structure, canvas spreads are suspended under the working area MAINLY to   3.____

    A. reduce noise   B. discourage crowds
    C. protect the structure   D. protect pedestrians

4. It is poor practice to hold a piece of wood in the hands or lap when tightening a screw in the wood.   4.____
This is for the reason that

    A. sufficient leverage cannot be obtained
    B. the screwdriver may bend
    C. the wood will probably split
    D. personal injury is likely to result

5. Steel helmets give workers the MOST protection from   5.____

    A. falling objects   B. eye injuries
    C. fire   D. electric shock

6. It is POOR practice to wear goggles   6.____

    A. when chipping stone
    B. when using a grinder
    C. while climbing or descending ladders
    D. when handling molten metal

7. When using a brace and bit to bore a hole completely through a partition, it is MOST important to   7.____

A. lean heavily on the brace and bit
B. maintain a steady turning speed all through the job
C. have the body in a position that will not be easily thrown off balance
D. reverse the direction of the bit at frequent intervals

8. Gloves should be used when handling 8.____

   A. lanterns   B. wooden rules
   C. heavy ropes   D. all small tools

Questions 9-16.

DIRECTIONS: Questions 9 through 16, inclusive, are based on the ladder safety rules given below. Read these rules fully before answering these items.

LADDER SAFETY RULES

When a ladder is placed on a slightly uneven supporting surface, use a flat piece of board or small wedge to even up the ladder feet. To secure the proper angle for resting a ladder, it should be placed so that the distance from the base of the ladder to the supporting wall is 1/4 the length of the ladder. To avoid overloading a ladder, only one person should work on a ladder at a time. Do not place a ladder in front of a door. When the top rung of a ladder rests against a pole, the ladder should be lashed securely. Clear loose stones or debris from the ground around the base of a ladder before climbing. While on a ladder, do not attempt to lean so that any part of the body, except arms or hands, extends more than 12 inches beyond the side rail. Always face the ladder when ascending or descending. When carrying ladders through buildings, watch for ceiling globes and lighting fixtures. Avoid the use of rolling ladders as scaffold supports.

9. A small wedge is used to 9.____

   A. even up the feet of a ladder resting on an uneven surface
   B. lock the wheels of a roller ladder
   C. secure the proper resting angle for a ladder
   D. secure a ladder against a pole

10. An 8 foot ladder resting against a wall should be so inclined that the distance between 10.____
    the base of the ladder and the wall is _____ feet.

    A. 2   B. 5   C. 7   D. 9

11. A ladder should be lashed securely when 11.____

    A. it is placed in front of a door
    B. loose stones are on the ground near the base of the ladder
    C. the top rung rests against a pole
    D. two people are working from the same ladder

12. Rolling ladders 12.____

    A. should be used for scaffold supports
    B. should not be used for scaffold supports
    C. are useful on uneven ground
    D. should be used against a pole

13. When carrying a ladder through a building, it is necessary to

   A. have two men to carry it
   B. carry the ladder vertically
   C. watch for ceiling globes
   D. face the ladder while carrying it

14. It is POOR practice to

   A. lash a ladder securely at any time
   B. clear debris from the base of a ladder before climbing
   C. even up the feet of a ladder resting on slightly uneven ground
   D. place a ladder in front of a door

15. A person on a ladder should NOT extend his head beyond the side rail by more than _____ inches.

   A. 12   B. 9   C. 7   D. 5

16. The MOST important reason for permitting only one person to work on a ladder at a time is that

   A. both could not face the ladder at one time
   B. the ladder will be overloaded
   C. time would be lost going up and down the ladder
   D. they would obstruct each other

17. Many portable electric power tools, such as electric drills, have a third conductor in the power lead which is used to connect the case of the tool to a grounded part of the electric outlet.
    The reason for this extra conductor is to

   A. have a spare wire in case one power wire should break
   B. strengthen the power lead so it cannot easily be damaged
   C. prevent the user of the tool from being shocked
   D. enable the tool to be used for long periods of time without overheating

18. Protective goggles should NOT be worn when

   A. standing on a ladder drilling a steel beam
   B. descending a ladder after completing a job
   C. chipping concrete near a third rail
   D. sharpening a cold chisel on a grinding stone

19. When the foot of an extension ladder, placed against a high wall, rests on a sidewalk or another such similar surface, it is advisable to tie a rope between the bottom rung of the ladder and a point on the wall opposite this rung.
    This is done to prevent

   A. people from walking under the ladder
   B. another worker from removing the ladder
   C. the ladder from vibrating when ascending or descending
   D. the foot of the ladder from slipping

20. In construction work, practically all accidents can be blamed on the

    A. failure of an individual to give close attention to the job assigned to him
    B. use of improper tools
    C. lack of cooperation among the men in a gang
    D. fact that an incompetent man was placed in a key position

21. If it is necessary for you to do some work with your hands under a piece of heavy equipment while a fellow worker lifts up and holds one end of it by means of a pinch bar, one important precaution you should take is to

    A. wear gloves
    B. watch the bar to be ready if it slips
    C. insert a temporary block to support the piece
    D. work as fast as possible

22. Employees of the transit system whose work requires them to enter upon the tracks in the subway are cautioned not to wear loose fitting clothing.
    The MOST important reason for this caution is that loose fitting clothing may

    A. interfere when men are using heavy tools
    B. catch on some projection of a passing train
    C. tear more easily than snug fitting clothing
    D. give insufficient protection against subway dust

23. The MOST important reason for insisting on neatness in maintenance quarters is that it

    A. keeps the men busy in slack periods
    B. prevents tools from becoming rusty
    C. makes a good impression on visitors and officials
    D. decreases the chances of accidents to employees

24. Maintenance workers whose duties require them to do certain types of work generally work in pairs.
    The LEAST likely of the following possible reasons for this practice is that

    A. some of the work requires two men
    B. the men can help each other in case of accident
    C. there is too much equipment for one man to carry
    D. it protects against vandalism

25. A foreman reprimands a helper for actions in violation of the rules and regulations.
    The BEST reaction of the helper in this situation is to

    A. tell the foreman that he was careful and that he did not take any chances
    B. explain that he took this action to save time
    C. keep quiet and accept the criticism
    D. demand that the foreman show him the rule he violated

KEY (CORRECT ANSWERS)

1. A
2. D
3. D
4. D
5. A

6. C
7. C
8. C
9. A
10. A

11. C
12. B
13. C
14. D
15. A

16. B
17. C
18. B
19. D
20. A

21. C
22. B
23. D
24. D
25. C

EXAMINATION SECTION
TEST 1

DIRECTIONS: Each question or incomplete statement is followed by several suggested answers or completions. Select the one that BEST answers the question or completes the statement. *PRINT THE LETTER OF THE CORRECT ANSWER IN THE SPACE AT THE RIGHT.*

1. At times there may be a conflict between employees' needs and agency goals. A supervisor's MAIN role in motivating employees in such circumstances is to try to
   A. develop good work habits among the employees whom he supervises
   B. emphasize the importance of material rewards such as merit increases
   C. keep careful records of employees' performance for possible disciplinary action
   D. reconcile employees' objectives with those of the public agency

   1.____

2. Organizations cannot function effectively without policies.
   However, when an organization imposes excessively detailed policy restrictions, it is MOST likely to lead to
   A. conflicts among individual employees
   B. a lack of adequate supervision
   C. a reduction of employee initiative
   D. a reliance on punitive discipline

   2.____

3. The PRIMARY responsibility for establishing good employee relations in the public service usually rests with
   A. employees   B. management
   C. civil service organizations   D. employee organizations

   3.____

4. At times, certain off-the-job conduct of public employees may be of concern to management. This concern stems from the fact that
   A. agency programs could be harmed by adverse publicity if employees' conduct is considered detrimental by the public
   B. fairness to all concerned is usually the major consideration in disciplinary cases
   C. public employees must meet higher standards than employees working in private industry
   D. public employees have high ethical standards and may participate in social action programs

   4.____

5. At one time or another, most employees ask for, or expect, special treatment. For a supervisor faced with this problem, the one of the following which is the MOST valid guideline is:
   A. According to the rules, a supervisor must give identical treatment to all his subordinates, regardless of the circumstances.

   5.____

59

B. Although all employees have equal rights, it is sometimes necessary to give an employee special treatment to meet an individual need.
C. It would damage morale if any employee were to receive special treatment, regardless of circumstances.
D. Since each employee has different needs, there is little reason to maintain general rules.

6. Mental health problems exist in many parts of our society and may also be found in the work setting.
   The BASIC role of the supervisor in relation to the mental health problems of his subordinates is to
   A. restrict himself solely to the taking of disciplinary measures, if warranted, and follow up carefully
   B. avoid involvement in personal matters
   C. identify mental health problems as early as possible
   D. resolve mental health problems through personal counseling

7. Supervisory expectation of high levels of employee performance, where such performance is possible, is MOST likely to lead to employees'
   A. expecting frequent praise and encouragement
   B. gaining a greater sense of satisfaction
   C. needing less detailed instructions than previously
   D. reducing their quantitative output

8. In public agencies, as elsewhere, supervisors sometimes compete with one another to increase their units' productivity.
   Of the following, the MAJOR disadvantage of such competition, from the general viewpoint of providing good public service, is that
   A. while individual employee effort will increase, unit productivity will decrease
   B. employees will be discouraged from sincere interest in their work
   C. the supervisors' competition may hinder the achievement of agency goals
   D. total payroll costs will increase as the activities of each unit increase

9. If employees are motivated primarily by material compensation, the amount of effort an individual employee will put into performing his work effectively will depend MAINLY upon how he perceives
   A. cooperation to be tied to successful effort
   B. the association between good work and increased compensation
   C. the public status of his particular position
   D. the supervisor's behavior in work situations

10. Cash awards to individual employees are sometimes used to encourage useful suggestions. However, some management experts believe that awards should involve some form of employee recognition other than cash.
    Which of the following reasons BEST supports opposition to using cash as a reward for worthwhile suggestions?

A. Cash awards cause employees to expend excessive time in making suggestions.
B. Taxpayer opposition to dash awards has increased following generous salary increases for public employees in recent years.
C. Public funds expended on awards leads to a poor image of public employees.
D. The use of cash awards raises the problem of deciding the monetary value of suggestions.

11. The BEST general rule for a supervisor to follow in giving praise and criticism is to
    A. criticize and praise publicly
    B. criticize publicly and praise privately
    C. praise and criticize privately
    D. praise publicly and criticize privately

12. An important step in designing an error-control policy is to determine the maximum number of errors that can be considered acceptable for the entire organization.
    Of the following, the MOST important factor in making such a decision is the
    A. number of clerical staff available to check for errors
    B. frequency of errors by supervisors
    C. human and material costs of errors
    D. number of errors that will become known to the public

13. When a supervisor tries to correct a situation where errors have been widespread, he should concentrate his efforts, and those of the employees involved, on
    A. avoiding future mistakes
    B. fixing appropriate blame
    C. preparing a written report
    D. determining fair penalties

14. When delegating work to a subordinate, a supervisor should ALWAYS tell the subordinate
    A. each step in the procedure for doing the work
    B. how much time to expend
    C. what is to be accomplished
    D. whether reports are necessary

15. The responsibilities of all employees should be clearly defined and understood. In addition, in order for employees to successfully fulfill their responsibilities, they should also GENERALLY be given
    A. written directives
    B. close supervision
    C. corresponding authority
    D. daily instructions

16. The one of the following types of training in which positive transfer of training to the actual work situation is MOST likely to take place is _____ training.
    A. conference
    B. demonstration
    C. classroom
    D. on-the-job

17. The type of training or instruction in which the subject matter is presented in small units called frames is known as
    A. programmed instruction
    B. reinforcement
    C. remediation
    D. skills training

18. In order to bring about maximum learning in a training situation, a supervisor acting as a trainer should attempt to create a setting in which
    A. all trainees experience a large amount of failure as an incentive
    B. all trainees experience a small amount of failure as an incentive
    C. each trainee experiences approximately the same amounts of success and failure
    D. each trainee experiences as much success and as little failure as possible

19. Assume that, in a training course given by an agency, the instructor conducts a brief quiz, on paper, toward the close of each session.
    From the point of view of maximizing learning, it would be BEST for the instructor to
    A. wait until the last session to provide the correct answers
    B. give the correct answers aloud immediately after each quiz
    C. permit trainees to take the questions home with them so that they can look up the answers
    D. wait until the next session to provide the correct answers

20. A supervisor, in the course of evaluating employees, should ALWAYS determine whether
    A. employees realize that their work is under scrutiny
    B. the ratings will be included in permanent records
    C. employees meet standards of performance
    D. his statements on the rating form are similar to those made by the previous supervisor

21. All of the following are legitimate objectives of employee performance reporting systems EXCEPT
    A. serving as a check on personnel policies such as job qualification requirements and placement techniques
    B. determining who is the least efficient worker among a large number of employees
    C. improving employee performance by identifying strong and weak points in individual performance
    D. developing standards of satisfactory performance

22. Studies of existing employee performance evaluation schemes have revealed a common tendency to construct guides in order to measure inferred traits.
    Of the following, the BEST example of an inferred trait is
    A. appearance   B. loyalty   C. accuracy   D. promptness

5 (#1)

23. Which of the following is MOST likely to be a positive influence in promoting common agreement at a staff conference?
    A. A mature, tolerant group of participants
    B. A strong chairman with firm opinions
    C. The normal differences of human personalities
    D. The urge to forcefully support one's views

23.____

24. Before holding a problem-solving conference, the conference leader sent to each invitee an announcement on which he listed the names of all invitees. His action in listing the names was
    A. *wise*, mainly because all invitees will know who has been invited, and can, if necessary, plan a proper approach
    B. *unwise*, mainly because certain invitees could form factions prior to the conference
    C. *unwise*, mainly because invitees might come to the conference in a belligerent mood if they had had interpersonal conflicts with other invitees
    D. *wise*, mainly because invitees who are antagonistic to each other could decide not to attend

24.____

25. Methods analysis is a detailed study of existing or proposed work methods for the purpose of improving agency operations.
    Of the following, it is MOST accurate to say that this type of study
    A. can sometimes be made informally by the experienced supervisor who can identify problems and suggest solutions
    B. is not suitable for studying the operations of a public agency
    C. will be successfully accomplished only if an outside organization reviews agency operations
    D. usually costs more to complete than is justified by the potential economies to be realized

25.____

KEY (CORRECT ANSWERS)

1.	D	11.	D
2.	C	12.	C
3.	B	13.	A
4.	A	14.	C
5.	B	15.	C
6.	C	16.	D
7.	B	17.	A
8.	C	18.	D
9.	B	19.	B
10.	D	20.	C

21.
22. B
23. A
24. A
25. A

TEST 2

DIRECTIONS: Each question or incomplete statement is followed by several suggested answers or completions. Select the one that BEST answers the question or completes the statement. *PRINT THE LETTER OF THE CORRECT ANSWER IN THE SPACE AT THE RIGHT.*

1. Present-day managerial practices advocate that adequate hierarchical levels of communication be maintained among all levels of management.
   Of the following, the BEST way to accomplish this is with
   A. intradepartmental memoranda only
   B. interdepartmental memoranda only
   C. periodic staff meetings, interdepartmental and intradepartmental memoranda
   D. interdepartmental and intradepartmental memoranda

   1.____

2. It is generally agreed upon that it is important to have effective communications in the unit so that everyone knows exactly what is expected of him.
   Of the following, the communications system which can assist in fulfilling this objective BEST is one which consists of
   A. written policies and procedures for administrative functions and verbal policies and procedures for professional functions
   B. written policies and procedures for professional and administrative functions
   C. verbal policies and procedures for professional and administrative functions
   D. verbal policies and procedures for professional functions

   2.____

3. If a department manager wishes to build an effective department, he MOST generally must
   A. be able to hire and fire as he feels necessary
   B. consider the total aspects of his job, his influence and the effects of his decisions
   C. have access to reasonable amounts of personnel and money with which to build his programs
   D. attend as many professional conferences as possible so that he can keep up-to-date with all the latest advances in the field

   3.____

4. Of the following, the factor which generally contributes MOST effectively to the performance of the unit is that the supervisor
   A. personally inspect the work of all employees
   B. fill orders at a faster rate than his subordinates
   C. have an exact knowledge of theory
   D. implement a program of professional development for his staff

   4.____

5. Administrative policies relate MOST closely to
   A. control of commodities and personnel
   B. general policies emanating from the central office
   C. fiscal management of the department only
   D. handling and dispensing of funds

   5.____

6. Part of being a good supervisor is to be able to develop an attitude towards employees which will motivate them to do their best on the job.
   The GOOD supervisor, therefore, should
   A. take an interest in subordinates, but not develop an all-consuming attitude in this area
   B. remain in an aloof position when dealing with employees
   C. be as close to subordinates as possible on the job
   D. take a complete interest in all the activities of subordinates, both on and off the job

7. The practice of a supervisor assigning an experienced employee to train new employees instead of training them himself is GENERALLY considered
   A. *undesirable*; the more experienced employee will resent being taken away from his regular job
   B. *desirable*; the supervisor can then devote more time to his regular duties
   C. *undesirable*; the more experienced employee is not working at the proper level to train new employees
   D. *desirable*; the more experienced employee is probably a better trainer than the supervisor

8. It is generally agreed that on-the-job training is MOST effective when new employees are
   A. provided with study manuals, standard operating procedures and other written materials to be studied for at least two weeks before the employees attempt to do the job
   B. shown how to do the job in detail, and then instructed to do the work under close supervision
   C. trained by an experienced worker for at least a week to make certain that the employees can do the job
   D. given work immediately which is checked at the end of each day

9. Employees sometimes form small informal groups, commonly called cliques. With regard to the effect of such groups on processing of the workload, the attitude a supervisor should take towards these cliques is that of
   A. *acceptance*, since they take the employees' minds off their work without wasting too much time
   B. *rejection*, since those workers inside the clique tend to do less work than the outsiders
   C. *acceptance*, since the supervisor is usually included in the clique
   D. *rejection*, since they are usually disliked by higher management

10. Of the following, the BEST statement regarding rules and regulations in a unit is that they
    A. are "necessary evils" to be tolerated by those at and above the first supervisory level only
    B. are stated in broad, indefinite terms so as to allow maximum amount of leeway in complying with them

C. must be understood by all employees in the unit
D. are primarily for management's needs since insurance regulations mandate them

11. It is sometimes considered desirable for a supervisor to survey the opinions of his employees before taking action on decisions affecting them.
Of the following the greatest DISADVANTAGE of following this approach is that the employees might
    A. use this opportunity to complain rather than to make constructive suggestions
    B. lose respect for their supervisor whom they feel cannot make his own decisions
    C. regard this as an attempt by the supervisor to get ideas for which he can later claim credit
    D. be resentful if their suggestions are not adopted

12. Of the following, the MOST important reason for keeping statements of duties of employees up-to-date is to
    A. serve as a basis of information for other governmental jurisdictions
    B. enable the department of personnel to develop job-related examinations
    C. differentiate between levels within the occupational groups
    D. enable each employee to know what his duties are

13. Of the following, the BEST way to evaluate the progress of a new subordinate is to
    A. compare the output of the new employee from week to week as to quantity and quality
    B. obtain the opinions of the new employee's co-workers
    C. test the new employee periodically to see how much he has learned
    D. hold frequent discussions with the employee focusing on his work

14. Of the following, a supervisor is LEAST likely to contribute to good morale in the unit if he
    A. encourages employees to increase their knowledge and proficiency in their work on their own time
    B. reprimands subordinates uniformly when infractions are committed
    C. refuses to accept explanations for mistakes regardless of who has made them or how serious they are
    D. compliments subordinates for superior work performance in the presence of their peers

15. The practice of promoting supervisors from within a given unit only, rather than from within the entire agency, may BEST be described as
    A. *desirable*, because the type of work in each unit generally is substantially different from all other units
    B. *undesirable*, since it will severely reduce the number of eligible from which to select a supervisor

C. *desirable*, since it enables each employee to know in advance the precise extent of promotion opportunities in his unit
D. *undesirable*, because it creates numerous administrative and budgetary difficulties

16. Of the following, the BEST way for a supervisor to make assignments GENERALLY is to
    A. give the easier assignments to employees with greater seniority
    B. give the difficult assignments to the employees with greater seniority
    C. make assignments according to the ability of each employee
    D. rotate the assignments among the employees

17. Assume that a supervisor makes a proposal through appropriate channels which would delegate final authority and responsibility to a subordinate employee for a major control function within the agency.
    According to current management theory, this proposal should be
    A. *adopted*, since this would enable the supervisor to devote more time to non-routine tasks
    B. *rejected*, since final responsibility for this high-level assignment may not properly be delegated to a subordinate employee
    C. *adopted*, since the assignment of increased responsibility to subordinate employees is a vital part of their development and training
    D. *rejected*, since the morale of the subordinate employees not selected for this assignment would be adversely affected

18. If it becomes necessary for a supervisor to improve the performance of a subordinate to assure the achievement of results according to plans, the BEST course of action, of the following, generally would be to
    A. emphasize the subordinate's strengths and try to motivate the employee to improve on those factors
    B. emphasize the subordinate's weak areas of performance and try to bring them up to an acceptable standard
    C. issue a memorandum to all employees warning that if performance does not improve, disciplinary measures will be taken
    D. transfer the subordinate to another section engaged in different work

19. A supervisor who specifies each phase of a job in detail supervises closely and permits very little discretion in performance of tasks GENERALLY
    A. provides motivation for his staff to produce more work
    B. finds that his subordinate make fewer mistakes than those with minimal supervision
    C. finds that his subordinates have little or no incentive to work any harder than necessary
    D. provides superior training opportunities for his employees

5 (#2)

20. Assume that you supervise two employees who do not get along well with each other. Their relationship has been continuously deteriorating. You decide to take steps to solve this problem by first determining the reason for their inability to get along with each other.
    This course of action is
    A. *desirable*, because their work is probably adversely affected by their differences
    B. *undesirable*, because your inquiries might be misinterpreted by the employees and cause resentment
    C. *desirable*, because you could then learn who is at fault for causing the deteriorating relationship and take appropriate disciplinary measures
    D. *undesirable*, because it is best to let them work their differences out between themselves

21. Routine procedures that have worked well in the past should be reviewed periodically by a supervisor MAINLY because
    A. they may have become outdated or in need of revision
    B. employees may dislike the procedures even though they have proven successful in the past
    C. these reviews are the main part of a supervisor's job
    D. this practice serves to give the supervisor an idea of how productive his subordinates are

22. Assume that an employee tells his supervisor about a grievance he has against a co-worker. The supervisor assures the employee that he will immediately take action to eliminate the grievance.
    The supervisor's attitude should be considered
    A. *correct*, because a good supervisor is one who can come to a quick decision
    B. *incorrect*, because the supervisor should have told the employee that he will investigate the grievance and then determine a future course of action
    C. *correct*, because the employee's morale will be higher, resulting in greater productivity
    D. *incorrect*, because the supervisor should remain uninvolved and let the employees settle grievances between themselves

23. If an employee's work output is low and of poor quality due to faulty work habits, the MOST constructive of the following ways for a supervisor to correct this situation *generally* is to
    A. discipline the employee
    B. transfer the employee to another unit
    C. provide additional training
    D. check the employee's work continuously

24. Assume that it becomes necessary for a supervisor to ask his staff to work overtime.
    Which one of the following techniques is MOST likely to win their willing cooperation to do this?

A. Point out that this is part of their job specification entitled "performs related work"
B. Explain the reason it is necessary for the employees to work overtime
C. Promise the employees special consideration regarding future leave matters
D. Warn that if the employees do not work overtime, they will face possible disciplinary action

25. If an employee's work performance has recently fallen below established minimum standards for quality and quantity, the threat of demotion or other disciplinary measures as an attempt to improve this employee's performance would probably be the MOST acceptable and effective course of action
    A. *only* after other more constructive measures have failed
    B. *if* applied uniformly to all employees as soon as performance falls below standard
    C. *only* if the employee understands that the threat will not actually be carried out
    D. *if* the employee is promised that, as soon as his work performance improves, he will be reinstated to his previous status

25._____

KEY (CORRECT ANSWERS)

1.	C		11.	D
2.	B		12.	D
3.	B		13.	A
4.	D		14.	C
5.	A		15.	B
6.	A		16.	C
7.	B		17.	B
8.	B		18.	B
9.	A		19.	C
10.	C		20.	A

21. A
22. B
23. C
24. B
25. A

TEST 3

DIRECTIONS: Each question or incomplete statement is followed by several suggested answers or completions. Select the one that BEST answers the question or completes the statement. *PRINT THE LETTER OF THE CORRECT ANSWER IN THE SPACE AT THE RIGHT.*

1. If, as a supervisor, it becomes necessary for you to assign an employee to supervise your unit during your vacation, it would generally be BEST to select the employee who
    A. is the best technician on the staff
    B. can get the work out smoothly, without friction
    C. has the most seniority
    D. is the most popular with the group

    1.____

2. Assume that, as a supervisor, your own work has accumulated to the point where you decide that it is desirable for you to delegate in order to meet your deadlines.
    The one of the following tasks which would be MOST appropriate to delegate to a subordinate is
    A. checking the work of the employees for accuracy
    B. attending a staff conference at which implementation of a new departmental policy will be discussed
    C. preparing a final report including a recommendation on purchase of expensive new laboratory equipment
    D. preparing final budget estimates for next year's budget

    2.____

3. Of the following actions, the one LEAST appropriate for you to take during an initial interview with a new employee is to
    A. find out about the experience and education of the new employee
    B. attempt to determine for what job in your unit the employee would best be suited
    C. tell the employee about his duties and responsibilities
    D. ascertain whether the employee will make good promotion material

    3.____

4. If it becomes necessary to reprimand a subordinate employee, the BEST of the following ways to do this is to
    A. ask the employee to stay after working hours and then reprimand him
    B. reprimand the employee immediately after the infraction has been committed
    C. take the employee aside and speak to him privately during regular working hours
    D. write a short memo to the employee warning that strict adherence to departmental policy and procedures is required of all employees

    4.____

5. If you, as a supervisor, believe that one of your subordinate employees has a serious problem, such as alcoholism or an emotional disturbance, which is adversely affecting his work, the BEST way to handle this situation *initially* would be to

    5.____

A. urge him to seek proper professional help before he is dismissed from his job
B. ignore it and let the employee work out the problem himself
C. suggest that the employee take an extended leave of absence until he can again function effectively
D. frankly tell the employee that unless his work improves, you will take disciplinary measures against him

6. Of the following, the BEST way to develop a subordinate's potential is to
   A. give him a fair chance to learn by doing
   B. assign him more than his share of work
   C. criticize only his work
   D. urge him to do his work rapidly

7. During a survey, an employee from another agency asks you to assist him on a job which would require a full day of your time.
   Of the following, the BEST immediate action for you to take is to
   A. refuse to assist him
   B. ask for compensation before doing it
   C. assist him promptly
   D. notify his department head

8. Of the following, the BEST way to handle an overly talkative subordinate is to
   A. have your superior talk to him about it
   B. have a subordinate talk to him about it
   C. talk to him about it in a group conference
   D. talk to him about it in private

9. While you are making a survey, a citizen questions you about the work you are doing.
   Of the following, the BEST thing to do is to
   A. answer the questions tactfully
   B. refuse to answer any questions
   C. advise him to write a letter to the main office
   D. answer the questions in double-talk

10. Respect for a supervisor is MOST likely to increase if he is
    A. morose   B. sporadic   C. vindictive   D. zealous

11. A subordinate who continuously bypasses his immediate supervisor for technical information should be
    A. reprimanded by his immediate supervisor
    B. ignored by his immediate supervisor
    C. given more difficult work to do
    D. given less difficult work to do

12. Complicated instructions should NOT be written
    A. accurately   B. lucidly   C. factually   D. verbosely

13. Of the following, the MOST important reason for checking a report is to
    A. check accuracy
    B. eliminate unnecessary sections
    C. catch mistakes
    D. check for delineation

14. Two subordinates under your supervision dislike each other to the extent that production is cut down.
    Your BEST action as a supervisor is to
    A. ignore the matter and hope for the best
    B. transfer the more aggressive man
    C. cut down on the workload
    D. talk to them together about the matter

15. One of the following characteristics which a supervisor should NOT display while explaining a job to a subordinate is
    A. enthusiasm   B. confidence   C. apathy   D. determination

16. Of the following, for BEST production of work, it should be assigned according to a person's
    A. attitude toward the work
    B. ability to do the work
    C. salary
    D. seniority

17. You receive an anonymous written complaint from a citizen about a subordinate who used abusive language.
    Of the following, your BEST course of action is to
    A. ignore the letter
    B. report it to your supervisor
    C. discuss the complaint with the subordinate privately
    D. keep the subordinate in the office

18. A supervisor should recognize that the way to get the BEST results from his instructions and assignments to the staff is to use
    A. a suggestive approach after he has decided exactly what is to be done and how
    B. the willing and cooperative staff members and avoid the hard-to-handle people
    C. care to select the persons most capable of carrying out the assignments
    D. an authoritative, non-nonsense tone when issuing instructions or giving assignments

19. As the supervisor of a unit, you find that you are spending too much of your time on routine tasks and not enough on coordinating the work of the staff or preparing necessary reports.
    Of the following, it would be MOST advisable for you to
    A. discard a great portion of the routine jobs done in the unit
    B. give some of the routine jobs to other members of the staff
    C. postpone the routine jobs and concentrate on coordinating the work of the staff
    D. delegate the job of coordinating the work to the most capable member of the staff

20. At times a supervisor may be called upon to train new employees. Suppose that you are giving such training in several sessions to be held on different days. During the first session, a trainee interrupts several times to ask questions at key points in your discussion.
    Of the following, the BEST way to handle this trainee is to
    A. advise him to pay closer attention so he can avoid asking too many questions
    B. tell him to listen without interrupting and he'll hear his questions answered
    C. answer his questions to show him that you know your field, but make a mental note that this trainee is a troublemaker
    D. answer each question fully and make certain he understands the answers

21. Employee errors can be reduced to a minimum by effective supervision and by training.
    Which of the following approaches used by a supervisor would usually be MOST effective in handling an employee who has made an avoidable and serious error for the first time?
    A. Tell the worker how other employees avoid making errors
    B. Analyze with the employee the situation leading to the error and then take whatever administrative or training steps are needed to avoid such errors
    C. Use this error as the basis for a staff meeting at which the employee's error is disclosed and discussed in an effort to improve the performance
    D. Urge the employee to modify his behavior in light of his mistake

22. Suppose that a particular staff member, formerly one of your most regular workers, has recently fallen into the habit of arriving a bit late to work several times a week. You feel that such a habit can grow consistently worse and spread to other staff members unless it is checked.
    Of the following, the BEST action for you to take, as the supervisor in charge of the unit, is to
    A. go immediately to your own supervisor, present the facts, and have this employee disciplined
    B. speak privately to this tardy employee, advise him of the need to improve his punctuality, and inform him that he'll be disciplined if late again
    C. talk to the co-worker with whom this late employee is most friendly, and ask the friend to help him solve his tardiness problem
    D. speak privately with this employee, and try to discover and deal with the reasons for the latenesses

23. A supervisor may make an assignment in the form of a request, a command, or a call for volunteers.
    It is LEAST desirable to make an assignment in the form of a request when
    A. an employee does not like the particular kind of assignment to be given
    B. the assignment requires working past the regular closing day
    C. an emergency has come up
    D. the assignment is not particularly pleasant for anybody

24. When you give a certain task that you normally perform yourself to one of your employees, it is MOST important that you
    A. lead the employee to believe that he has been chosen above others to perform this job
    B. describe the job as important even though it is merely a routine task
    C. explain the job that needs to be accomplished, but always let the employee decide how to do it
    D. tell the employee why you are delegating the job to him and explain exactly what he is to do

25. A supervisor when instructing new trainees in the routine of his unit should include a description of the department's overall objectives and programs in order to
    A. insure that individual work assignments will be completed satisfactorily
    B. create a favorable impression of his supervisory capabilities
    C. develop a better understanding of the purposes behind work assignments
    D. produce an immediate feeling of group cooperation

KEY (CORRECT ANSWERS)

1.	B		11.	A
2.	A		12.	D
3.	D		13.	C
4.	C		14.	D
5.	A		15.	C
6.	A		16.	B
7.	A		17.	C
8.	D		18.	C
9.	A		19.	B
10.	D		20.	D

21.	B
22.	D
23.	A
24.	D
25.	C

TEST 4

DIRECTIONS: Each question or incomplete statement is followed by several suggested answers or completions. Select the one that BEST answers the question or completes the statement. *PRINT THE LETTER OF THE CORRECT ANSWER IN THE SPACE AT THE RIGHT.*

1. An integral part of every supervisor's job is getting his ideas or instructions across to his staff.
   The extent of his success, if he has a reasonably competent staff, is PRIMARILY dependent on the
   A. interest of the employee
   B. intelligence of the employee
   C. reasoning behind the ideas or instructions
   D. presentation of the ideas or instructions

   1.____

2. Generally, what is the FIRST action the supervisor should take when an employee approaches him with a complaint?
   A. Review the employee's recent performance with him
   B. Use the complaint as a basis to discuss improvement of procedures
   C. Find out from the employee the details of the complaint
   D. Advise the employee to take his complaint to the head of the department

   2.____

3. Of the following, which is NOT usually considered one of the purposes of counseling an employee after an evaluation of his performance?
   A. Explaining the performance standards used by the supervisor
   B. Discussing necessary discipline action to be taken
   C. Emphasizing the employee's strengths and weaknesses
   D. Planning better utilization of the employee's strengths

   3.____

4. Assume that a supervisor, when reviewing a decision reached by one of his subordinates, finds the decision incorrect.
   Under these circumstances, it would be MOST desirable for the supervisor to
   A. correct the decision and inform the subordinate of this at a staff meeting
   B. correct the decision and suggest a more detailed analysis in the future
   C. help the employee find the reason for the correct decision
   D. refrain from assigning this type of a problem to the employee

   4.____

5. An IMPORTANT characteristic of a good supervisor is his ability to
   A. be a stern disciplinarian   B. put off the settling of grievances
   C. solve problems   D. find fault in individuals

   5.____

6. A new supervisor will BEST obtain the respect of the men assigned to him if he
   A. makes decisions rapidly and sticks to the, regardless of whether they are right or wrong
   B. makes decisions rapidly and then changes them just as rapidly if the decisions are wrong
   C. does not make any decisions unless he is absolutely sure that they are right
   D. makes his decisions after considering carefully all available information

   6.____

7. A newly appointed worker is operating at a level of performance below that of the other employees.
   In this situation, a supervisor should FIRST
   A. lower the acceptable standard for the new man
   B. find out why the new man cannot do as well as the others
   C. advise the new worker he will be dropped from the payroll at the end of the probationary period
   D. assign another new worker to assist the first man

8. Assume that you have to instruct a new man on a specific departmental operation. The new man seems unsure of what you have said.
   Of the following, the BEST way for you to determine whether the man has understood you is to
   A. have the man explain the operation to you in his own words
   B. repeat your explanation to him slowly
   C. repeat your explanation to him, using simpler wording
   D. emphasize the important parts of the operation to him

9. A supervisor realizes that he has taken an instantaneous dislike to a new worker assigned to him.
   The BEST course of action for the supervisor to take in this case is to
   A. be especially observant of the new worker's actions
   B. request that the new worker be reassigned
   C. make a special effort to be fair to the new worker
   D. ask to be transferred himself

10. A supervisor gives detailed instructions to his men as to how a certain type of job is to be done.
    One ADVANTAGE of this practice is that this will
    A. result in a more flexible operation
    B. standardize operations
    C. encourage new men to learn
    D. encourage initiative to learn

11. Of the following the one that would MOST likely be the result of poor planning is:
    A. Omissions are discovered after the work is completed
    B. During the course of normal inspection, a meter is found to be inaccessible
    C. An inspector completes his assignments for that day ahead of schedule
    D. A problem arises during an inspection and prevents an inspector from completing his day's assignments

12. Of the following, the BEST way for a supervisor to maintain good employee morale is for the supervisor to
    A. avoid correcting the employee when he makes mistakes
    B. continually praise the employee's work even when it is of average quality
    C. show that he is willing to assist in solving the employee's problems
    D. accept the employee's excuses for failure even though the excuses are not valid

13. A supervisor takes time to explain to his men why a departmental order has been issued.
    This practice is
    A. *good*, mainly because without this explanation the men will not be able to carry out the order
    B. *bad*, mainly because time will be wasted for no useful purpose
    C. *good*, because understanding the reasons behind an order will lead to more effective carrying out of the order
    D. *bad*, because men will then question every order that they receive

14. Of the following, the MOST important responsibility of a supervisor in charge of a section is to
    A. establish close personal relationships with each of his subordinates in the section
    B. insure that each subordinate in the section knows the full range of his duties and responsibilities
    C. maintain friendly relations with his immediate supervisor
    D. protect his subordinate from criticism from any source

15. The BEST way to get a good work output from employees is to
    A. hold over them the threat of disciplinary action or removal
    B. maintain a steady, unrelenting pressure on them
    C. show them that you can do anything they can do faster and better
    D. win their respect and liking, so they want to work for you

KEY (CORRECT ANSWERS)

1.	A	6.	D	11.	A
2.	C	7.	B	12.	C
3.	A	8.	A	13.	C
4.	C	9.	C	14.	B
5.	C	10.	B	15.	D

PHILOSOPHY, PRINCIPLES, PRACTICES, AND TECHNICS
OF
SUPERVISION, ADMINISTRATION, MANAGEMENT, AND ORGANIZATION

TABLE OF CONTENTS

	Page
MEANING OF SUPERVISION	1
THE OLD AND THE NEW SUPERVISION	1
THE EIGHT (8) BASIC PRINCIPLES OF THE NEW SUPERVISION	1
I. Principle of Responsibility	1
II. Principle of Authority	2
III. Principle of Self-Growth	2
IV. Principle of Individual Worth	2
V. Principle of Creative Leadership	2
VI. Principle of Success and Failure	2
VII. Principle of Science	3
VIII. Principle of Cooperation	3
WHAT IS ADMINISTRATION?	3
I. Practices Commonly Classed as "Supervisory"	3
II. Practices Commonly Classed as "Administrative"	3
III. Practices Commonly Classed as Both "Supervisory" and "Administrative"	4
RESPONSIBILITIES OF THE SUPERVISOR	4
COMPETENCIES OF THE SUPERVISOR	4
THE PROFESSIONAL SUPERVISOR-EMPLOYEE RELATIONSHIP	4
MINI-TEXT IN SUPERVISION, ADMINISTRATION, MANAGEMENT, AND ORGANIZATION	5
I. Brief Highlights	5
A. Levels of Management	6
B. What the Supervisor Must Learn	6
C. A Definition of Supervision	6
D. Elements of the Team Concept	6
E. Principles of Organization	6
F. The Four Important Parts of Every Job	7
G. Principles of Delegation	7
H. Principles of Effective Communications	7
I. Principles of Work Improvement	7
J. Areas of Job Improvement	7
K. Seven Key Points in Making Improvements	8

	L.	Corrective Techniques for Job Improvement	8
	M.	A Planning Checklist	8
	N.	Five Characteristics of Good Directions	9
	O.	Types of Directions	9
	P.	Controls	9
	Q.	Orienting the New Employee	9
	R.	Checklist for Orienting New Employees	9
	S.	Principles of Learning	10
	T.	Causes of Poor Performance	10
	U.	Four Major Steps in On-the-Job Instructions	10
	V.	Employees Want Five Things	10
	W.	Some Don'ts in Regard to Praise	11
	X.	How to Gain Your Workers' Confidence	11
	Y.	Sources of Employee Problems	11
	Z.	The Supervisor's Key to Discipline	11
	AA.	Five Important Processes of Management	12
	BB.	When the Supervisor Fails to Plan	12
	CC.	Fourteen General Principles of Management	12
	DD.	Change	12
II.	Brief Topical Summaries		13
	A.	Who/What is the Supervisor?	13
	B.	The Sociology of Work	13
	C.	Principles and Practices of Supervision	14
	D.	Dynamic Leadership	14
	E.	Processes for Solving Problems	15
	F.	Training for Results	15
	G.	Health, Safety, and Accident Prevention	16
	H.	Equal Employment Opportunity	16
	I.	Improving Communications	16
	J.	Self-Development	17
	K.	Teaching and Training	17
		1. The Teaching Process	17
		a. Preparation	17
		b. Presentation	18
		c. Summary	18
		d. Application	18
		e. Evaluation	18
		2. Teaching Methods	18
		a. Lecture	18
		b. Discussion	18
		c. Demonstration	19
		d. Performance	19
		e. Which Method to Use	19

PHILOSOPHY, PRINCIPLES, PRACTICES, AND TECHNICS OF SUPERVISION, ADMINISTRATION, MANAGEMENT, AND ORGANIZATION

MEANING OF SUPERVISION

The extension of the democratic philosophy has been accompanied by an extension in the scope of supervision. Modern leaders and supervisors no longer think of supervision in the narrow sense of being confined chiefly to visiting employees, supplying materials, or rating the staff. They regard supervision as being intimately related to all the concerned agencies of society, they speak of the supervisor's function in terms of "growth," rather than the "improvement" of employees.

This modern concept of supervision may be defined as follows: Supervision is leadership and the development of leadership within groups which are cooperatively engaged in inspection, research, training, guidance, and evaluation.

THE OLD AND THE NEW SUPERVISION

TRADITIONAL
1. Inspection
2. Focused on the employee
3. Visitation
4. Random and haphazard
5. Imposed and authoritarian
6. One person usually

MODERN
1. Study and analysis
2. Focused on aims, materials, methods, supervisors, employees, environment
3. Demonstrations, intervisitation, workshops, directed reading, bulletins, etc.
4. Definitely organized and planned (scientific)
5. Cooperative and democratic
6. Many persons involved (creative)

THE EIGHT (8) BASIC PRINCIPLES OF THE NEW SUPERVISION

I. Principle of Responsibility
   Authority to act and responsibility for acting must be joined.
   A. If you give responsibility, give authority.
   B. Define employee duties clearly.
   C. Protect employees from criticism by others.
   D. Recognize the rights as well as obligations of employees.
   E. Achieve the aims of a democratic society insofar as it is possible within the area of your work.
   F. Establish a situation favorable to training and learning.
   G. Accept ultimate responsibility for everything done in your section, unit, office, division, department.
   H. Good administration and good supervision are inseparable.

II. Principle of Authority
The success of the supervisor is measured by the extent to which the power of authority is not used.
- A. Exercise simplicity and informality in supervision
- B. Use the simplest machinery of supervision
- C. If it is good for the organization as a whole, it is probably justified.
- D. Seldom be arbitrary or authoritative.
- E. Do not base your work on the power of position or of personality.
- F. Permit and encourage the free expression of opinions.

III. Principle of Self-Growth
The success of the supervisor is measured by the extent to which, and the speed with which, he is no longer needed.
- A. Base criticism on principles, not on specifics.
- B. Point out higher activities to employees.
- C. Train for self-thinking by employees to meet new situations.
- D. Stimulate initiative, self-reliance, and individual responsibility
- E. Concentrate on stimulating the growth of employees rather than on removing defects.

IV. Principle of Individual Worth
Respect for the individual is a paramount consideration in supervision.
- A. Be human and sympathetic in dealing with employees.
- B. Don't nag about things to be done.
- C. Recognize the individual differences among employees and seek opportunities to permit best expression of each personality.

V. Principle of Creative Leadership
The best supervision is that which is not apparent to the employee.
- A. Stimulate, don't drive employees to creative action.
- B. Emphasize doing good things.
- C. Encourage employees to do what they do best.
- D. Do not be too greatly concerned with details of subject or method.
- E. Do not be concerned exclusively with immediate problems and activities.
- F. Reveal higher activities and make them both desired and maximally possible.
- G. Determine procedures in the light of each situation but see that these are derived from a sound basic philosophy.
- H. Aid, inspire, and lead so as to liberate the creative spirit latent in all good employees.

VI. Principle of Success and Failure
There are no unsuccessful employees, only unsuccessful supervisors who have failed to give proper leadership.
- A. Adapt suggestions to the capacities, attitudes, and prejudices of employees.
- B. Be gradual, be progressive, be persistent.
- C. Help the employee find the general principle; have the employee apply his own problem to the general principle.
- D. Give adequate appreciation for good work and honest effort.
- E. Anticipate employee difficulties and help to prevent them.
- F. Encourage employees to do the desirable things they will do anyway.
- G. Judge your supervision by the results it secures.

VII. Principle of Science
Successful supervision is scientific, objective, and experimental. It is based on facts, not on prejudices.
  A. Be cumulative in results.
  B. Never divorce your suggestions from the goals of training.
  C. Don't be impatient of results.
  D. Keep all matters on a professional, not a personal, level.
  E. Do not be concerned exclusively with immediate problems and activities.
  F. Use objective means of determining achievement and rating where possible.

VIII. Principle of Cooperation
Supervision is a cooperative enterprise between supervisor and employee.
  A. Begin with conditions as they are.
  B. Ask opinions of all involved when formulating policies.
  C. Organization is as good as its weakest link.
  D. Let employees help to determine policies and department programs.
  E. Be approachable and accessible—physically and mentally.
  F. Develop pleasant social relationships.

WHAT IS ADMINISTRATION

Administration is concerned with providing the environment, the material facilities, and the operational procedures that will promote the maximum growth and development of supervisors and employees. (Organization is an aspect and a concomitant of administration.)

There is no sharp line of demarcation between supervision and administration; these functions are intimately interrelated and, often, overlapping. They are complementary activities.

I. Practices Commonly Classed as "Supervisory"
  A. Conducting employees' conferences
  B. Visiting sections, units, offices, divisions, departments
  C. Arranging for demonstrations
  D. Examining plans
  E. Suggesting professional reading
  F. Interpreting bulletins
  G. Recommending in-service training courses
  H. Encouraging experimentation
  I. Appraising employee morale
  J. Providing for intervisitation

II. Practices Commonly Classified as "Administrative"
  A. Management of the office
  B. Arrangement of schedules for extra duties
  C. Assignment of rooms or areas
  D. Distribution of supplies
  E. Keeping records and reports
  F. Care of audio-visual materials
  G. Keeping inventory records
  H. Checking record cards and books

I. Programming special activities
J. Checking on the attendance and punctuality of employees

III. Practices Commonly Classified as Both "Supervisory" and "Administrative"
A. Program construction
B. Testing or evaluating outcomes
C. Personnel accounting
D. Ordering instructional materials

RESPONSIBILITIES OF THE SUPERVISOR

A person employed in a supervisory capacity must constantly be able to improve his own efficiency and ability. He represent the employer to the employees and only continuous self-examination can make him a capable supervisor.

Leadership and training are the supervisor's responsibility. An efficient working unit is one in which the employees work with the supervisor. It is his job to bring out the best in his employees. He must always be relaxed, courteous, and calm in his association with his employees. Their feelings are important, and a harsh attitude does not develop the most efficient employees.

COMPETENCES OF THE SUPERVISOR

I. Complete knowledge of the duties and responsibilities of his position.
II. To be able to organize a job, plan ahead, and carry through.
III. To have self-confidence and initiative.
IV. To be able to handle the unexpected situation and make quick decisions.
V. To be able to properly train subordinates in the positions they are best suited for.
VI. To be able to keep good human relations among his subordinates.
VII. To be able to keep good human relations between his subordinates and himself and to earn their respect and trust.

THE PROFESSIONAL SUPERVISOR-EMPLOYEE RELATIONSHIP

There are two kinds of efficiency: one kind is only apparent and is produced in organizations through the exercise of mere discipline; this is but a simulation of the second, or true, efficiency which springs from spontaneous cooperation. If you are a manager, no matter how great or small your responsibility, it is your job, in the final analysis, to create and develop this involuntary cooperation among the people whom you supervise. For, no matter how powerful a combination of money, machines, and materials a company may have, this is a dead and sterile thing without a team of willing, thinking, and articulate people to guide it.

The following 21 points are presented as indicative of the exemplary basic relationship that should exist between supervisor and employee:

1. Each person wants to be liked and respected by his fellow employee and wants to be treated with consideration and respect by his superior.
2. The most competent employee will make an error. However, in a unit where good relations exist between the supervisor and his employees, tenseness and fear do not exist. Thus, errors are not hidden or covered up, and the efficiency of a unit is not impaired.

3. Subordinates resent rules, regulations, or orders that are unreasonable or unexplained.
4. Subordinates are quick to resent unfairness, harshness, injustices, and favoritism.
5. An employee will accept responsibility if he knows that he will be complimented for a job well done, and not too harshly chastised for failure; that his supervisor will check the cause of the failure, and, if it was the supervisor's fault, he will assume the blame therefore. If it was the employee's fault, his supervisor will explain the correct method or means of handling the responsibility.
6. An employee wants to receive credit for a suggestion he has made, that is used. If a suggestion cannot be used, the employee is entitled to an explanation. The supervisor should not say "no" and close the subject.
7. Fear and worry slow up a worker's ability. Poor working environment can impair his physical and mental health. A good supervisor avoids forceful methods, threats, and arguments to get a job done.
8. A forceful supervisor is able to train his employees individually and as a team, and is able to motivate them in the proper channels.
9. A mature supervisor is able to properly evaluate his subordinates and to keep them happy and satisfied.
10. A sensitive supervisor will never patronize his subordinates.
11. A worthy supervisor will respect his employees' confidences.
12. Definite and clear-cut responsibilities should be assigned to each executive.
13. Responsibility should always be coupled with corresponding authority.
14. No change should be made in the scope or responsibilities of a position without a definite understanding to that effect on the part of all persons concerned.
15. No executive or employee, occupying a single position in the organization, should be subject to definite orders from more than one source.
16. Orders should never be given to subordinates over the head of a responsible executive. Rather than do this, the officer in question should be supplanted.
17. Criticisms of subordinates should, whoever possible, be made privately, and in no case should a subordinate be criticized in the presence of executives or employees of equal or lower rank.
18. No dispute or difference between executives or employees as to authority or responsibilities should be considered too trivial for prompt and careful adjudication.
19. Promotions, wage changes, and disciplinary action should always be approved by the executive immediately superior to the one directly responsible.
20. No executive or employee should ever be required, or expected, to be at the same time an assistant to, and critic of, another.
21. Any executive whose work is subject to regular inspection should, wherever practicable, be given the assistance and facilities necessary to enable him to maintain an independent check of the quality of his work.

MINI-TEXT IN SUPERVISION, ADMINISTRATION, MANAGEMENT, AND ORGANIZATION

I. Brief Highlights

Listed concisely and sequentially are major headings and important data in the field for quick recall and review.

A. Levels of Management
Any organization of some size has several levels of management. In terms of a ladder, the levels are:

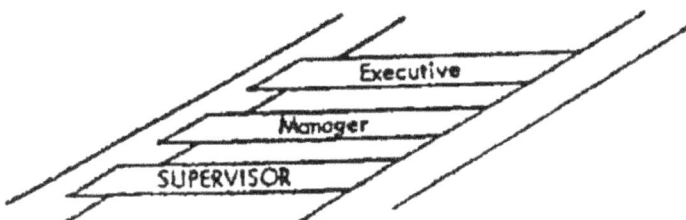

The first level is very important because it is the beginning point of management leadership.

B. What the Supervisor Must Learn
A supervisor must learn to:
1. Deal with people and their differences
2. Get the job done through people
3. Recognize the problems when they exist
4. Overcome obstacles to good performance
5. Evaluate the performance of people
6. Check his own performance in terms of accomplishment

C. A Definition of Supervisor
The term supervisor means any individual having authority, in the interests of the employer, to hire, transfer, suspend, lay-off, recall, promote, discharge, assign, reward, or discipline other employees or responsibility to direct them, or to adjust their grievances, or effectively to recommend such action, if, in connection with the foregoing, exercise of such authority is not of a merely routine or clerical nature but requires the use of independent judgment.

D. Elements of the Team Concept
What is involved in teamwork? The component parts are:
1. Members
2. A leader
3. Goals
4. Plans
5. Cooperation
6. Spirit

E. Principles of Organization
1. A team member must know what his job is.
2. Be sure that the nature and scope of a job are understood.
3. Authority and responsibility should be carefully spelled out.
4. A supervisor should be permitted to make the maximum number of decisions affecting his employees.
5. Employees should report to only one supervisor.
6. A supervisor should direct only as many employees as he can handle effectively.
7. An organization plan should be flexible.

8. Inspection and performance of work should be separate.
9. Organizational problems should receive immediate attention.
10. Assign work in line with ability and experience.

F. The Four Important Parts of Every Job
1. Inherent in every job is the *accountability* for results.
2. A second set of factors in every job is *responsibilities*.
3. Along with duties and responsibilities one must have the *authority* to act within certain limits without obtaining permission to proceed.
4. No job exists in a vacuum. The supervisor is surrounded by key *relationships*.

G. Principles of Delegation
Where work is delegated for the first time, the supervisor should think in terms of these questions:
1. Who is best qualified to do this?
2. Can an employee improve his abilities by doing this?
3. How long should an employee spend on this?
4. Are there any special problems for which he will need guidance?
5. How broad a delegation can I make?

H. Principles of Effective Communications
1. Determine the media.
2. To whom directed?
3. Identification and source authority.
4. Is communication understood?

I. Principles of Work Improvement
1. Most people usually do only the work which is assigned to them.
2. Workers are likely to fit assigned work into the time available to perform it.
3. A good workload usually stimulates output.
4. People usually do their best work when they know that results will be reviewed or inspected.
5. Employees usually feel that someone else is responsible for conditions of work, workplace layout, job methods, type of tools/equipment, and other such factors.
6. Employees are usually defensive about their job security.
7. Employees have natural resistance to change.
8. Employees can support or destroy a supervisor.
9. A supervisor usually earns the respect of his people through his personal example of diligence and efficiency.

J. Areas of Job Improvement
The areas of job improvement are quite numerous, but the most common ones which a supervisor can identify and utilize are:
1. Departmental layout
2. Flow of work
3. Workplace layout
4. Utilization of manpower
5. Work methods
6. Materials handling

7. Utilization
8. Motion economy

K. Seven Key Points in Making Improvements
   1. Select the job to be improved
   2. Study how it is being done now
   3. Question the present method
   4. Determine actions to be taken
   5. Chart proposed method
   6. Get approval and apply
   7. Solicit worker participation

I. Corrective Techniques of Job Improvement
   Specific Problems
   1. Size of workload
   2. Inability to meet schedules
   3. Strain and fatigue
   4. Improper use of men and skills
   5. Waste, poor quality, unsafe conditions
   6. Bottleneck conditions that hinder output
   7. Poor utilization of equipment and machine
   8. Efficiency and productivity of labor

   General Improvement
   1. Departmental layout
   2. Flow of work
   3. Work plan layout
   4. Utilization of manpower
   5. Work methods
   6. Materials handling
   7. Utilization of equipment
   8. Motion economy

   Corrective Techniques
   1. Study with scale model
   2. Flow chart study
   3. Motion analysis
   4. Comparison of units produced to standard allowance
   5. Methods analysis
   6. Flow chart and equipment study
   7. Down time vs. running time
   8. Motion analysis

M. A Planning Checklist
   1. Objectives
   2. Controls
   3. Delegations
   4. Communications
   5. Resources
   6. Manpower

7. Equipment
8. Supplies and materials
9. Utilization of time
10. Safety
11. Money
12. Work
13. Timing of improvements

N. Five Characteristics of Good Directions
In order to get results, directions must be:
1. Possible of accomplishment
2. Agreeable with worker interests
3. Related to mission
4. Planned and complete
5. Unmistakably clear

O. Types of Directions
1. Demands or direct orders
2. Requests
3. Suggestion or implication
4. volunteering

P. Controls
A typical listing of the overall areas in which the supervisor should establish controls might be:
1. Manpower
2. Materials
3. Quality of work
4. Quantity of work
5. Time
6. Space
7. Money
8. Methods

Q. Orienting the New Employee
1. Prepare for him
2. Welcome the new employee
3. Orientation for the job
4. Follow-up

R. Checklist for Orienting New Employees   Yes   No
1. Do you appreciate the feelings of new employees
   when they first report for work?   ___   ___
2. Are you aware of the fact that the new employee must
   make a big adjustment to his job?   ___   ___
3. Have you given him good reasons for liking the job and
   the organization?   ___   ___
4. Have you prepared for his first day on the job?   ___   ___
5. Did you welcome him cordially and make him feel needed?   ___   ___

		Yes	No
6.	Did you establish rapport with him so that he feels free to talk and discuss matters with you?	___	___
7.	Did you explain his job to him and his relationship to you?	___	___
8.	Does he know that his work will be evaluated periodically on a basis that is fair and objective?	___	___
9.	Did you introduce him to his fellow workers in such a way that they are likely to accept him?	___	___
10.	Does he know what employee benefits he will receive?	___	___
11.	Does he understand the importance of being on the job and what to do if he must leave his duty station?	___	___
12.	Has he been impressed with the importance of accident prevention and safe practice?	___	___
13.	Does he generally know his way around the department?	___	___
14.	Is he under the guidance of a sponsor who will teach the right way of doing things?	___	___
15.	Do you plan to follow-up so that he will continue to adjust successfully to his job?	___	___

S. Principles of Learning
1. Motivation
2. Demonstration or explanation
3. Practice

T. Causes of Poor Performance
1. Improper training for job
2. Wrong tools
3. Inadequate directions
4. Lack of supervisory follow-up
5. Poor communications
6. Lack of standards of performance
7. Wrong work habits
8. Low morale
9. Other

U. Four Major Steps in On-The-Job Instruction
1. Prepare the worker
2. Present the operation
3. Tryout performance
4. Follow-up

V. Employees Want Five Things
1. Security
2. Opportunity
3. Recognition
4. Inclusion
5. Expression

W. Some Don'ts in Regard to Praise
1. Don't praise a person for something he hasn't done.
2. Don't praise a person unless you can be sincere.
3. Don't be sparing in praise just because your superior withholds it from you.
4. Don't let too much time elapse between good performance and recognition of it

X. How to Gain Your Workers' Confidence
Methods of developing confidence include such things as:
1. Knowing the interests, habits, hobbies of employees
2. Admitting your own inadequacies
3. Sharing and telling of confidence in others
4. Supporting people when they are in trouble
5. Delegating matters that can be well handled
6. Being frank and straightforward about problems and working conditions
7. Encouraging others to bring their problems to you
8. Taking action on problems which impede worker progress

Y. Sources of Employee Problems
On-the-job causes might be such things as:
1. A feeling that favoritism is exercised in assignments
2. Assignment of overtime
3. An undue amount of supervision
4. Changing methods or systems
5. Stealing of ideas or trade secrets
6. Lack of interest in job
7. Threat of reduction in force
8. Ignorance or lack of communications
9. Poor equipment
10. Lack of knowing how supervisor feels toward employee
11. Shift assignments

Off-the-job problems might have to do with:
1. Health
2. Finances
3. Housing
4. Family

Z. The Supervisor's Key to Discipline
There are several key points about discipline which the supervisor should keep in mind:
1. Job discipline is one of the disciplines of life and is directed by the supervisor.
2. It is more important to correct an employee fault than to fix blame for it.
3. Employee performance is affected by problems both on the job and off.
4. Sudden or abrupt changes in behavior can be indications of important employee problems.
5. Problems should be dealt with as soon as possible after they are identified.
6. The attitude of the supervisor may have more to do with solving problems than the techniques of problem solving.
7. Correction of employee behavior should be resorted to only after the supervisor is sure that training or counseling will not be helpful.

8. Be sure to document your disciplinary actions.
9. Make sure that you are disciplining on the basis of facts rather than personal feelings.
10. Take each disciplinary step in order, being careful not to make snap judgments, or decisions based on impatience.

AA. Five Important Processes of Management
1. Planning
2. Organizing
3. Scheduling
4. Controlling
5. Motivating

BB. When the Supervisor Fails to Plan
1. Supervisor creates impression of not knowing his job
2. May lead to excessive overtime
3. Job runs itself—supervisor lacks control
4. Deadlines and appointments missed
5. Parts of the work go undone
6. Work interrupted by emergencies
7. Sets a bad example
8. Uneven workload creates peaks and valleys
9. Too much time on minor details at expense of more important tasks

CC. Fourteen General Principles of Management
1. Division of work
2. Authority and responsibility
3. Discipline
4. Unity of command
5. Unity of direction
6. Subordination of individual interest to general interest
7. Remuneration of personnel
8. Centralization
9. Scalar chain
10. Order
11. Equity
12. Stability of tenure of personnel
13. Initiative
14. Esprit de corps

DD. Change

Bringing about change is perhaps attempted more often, and yet less well understood, than anything else the supervisor does. How do people generally react to change? (People tend to resist change that is imposed upon them by other individuals or circumstances.

Change is characteristic of every situation. It is a part of every real endeavor where the efforts of people are concerned.

1. Why do people resist change?
   People may resist change because of:
   a. Fear of the unknown
   b. Implied criticism
   c. Unpleasant experiences in the past
   d. Fear of loss of status
   e. Threat to the ego
   f. Fear of loss of economic stability

2. How can we best overcome the resistance to change?
   In initiating change, take these steps:
   a. Get ready to sell
   b. Identify sources of help
   c. Anticipate objections
   d. Sell benefits
   e. Listen in depth
   f. Follow up

II. Brief Topical Summaries

   A. Who/What is the Supervisor?
      1. The supervisor is often called the "highest level employee and the lowest level manager."
      2. A supervisor is a member of both management and the work group. He acts as a bridge between the two.
      3. Most problems in supervision are in the area of human relations, or people problems.
      4. Employees expect: Respect, opportunity to learn and to advance, and a sense of belonging, and so forth.
      5. Supervisors are responsible for directing people and organizing work. Planning is of paramount importance.
      6. A position description is a set of duties and responsibilities inherent to a given position.
      7. It is important to keep the position description up-to-date and to provide each employee with his own copy.

   B. The Sociology of Work
      1. People are alike in many ways; however, each individual is unique.
      2. The supervisor is challenged in getting to know employee differences. Acquiring skills in evaluating individuals is an asset.
      3. Maintaining meaningful working relationships in the organization is of great importance.
      4. The supervisor has an obligation to help individuals to develop to their fullest potential.
      5. Job rotation on a planned basis helps to build versatility and to maintain interest and enthusiasm in work groups.
      6. Cross training (job rotation) provides backup skills.

7. The supervisor can help reduce tension by maintaining a sense of humor, providing guidance to employees, and by making reasonable and timely decisions. Employees respond favorably to working under reasonably predictable circumstances.
8. Change is characteristic of all managerial behavior. The supervisor must adjust to changes in procedures, new methods, technological changes, and to a number of new and sometimes challenging situations.
9. To overcome the natural tendency for people to resist change, the supervisor should become more skillful in initiating change.

C. Principles and Practices of Supervision
1. Employees should be required to answer to only one superior.
2. A supervisor can effectively direct only a limited number of employees, depending upon the complexity, variety, and proximity of the jobs involved.
3. The organizational chart presents the organization in graphic form. It reflects lines of authority and responsibility as well as interrelationships of units within the organization.
4. Distribution of work can be improved through an analysis using the "Work Distribution Chart."
5. The "Work Distribution Chart" reflects the division of work within a unit in understandable form.
6. When related tasks are given to an employee, he has a better chance of increasing his skills through training.
7. The individual who is given the responsibility for tasks must also be given the appropriate authority to insure adequate results.
8. The supervisor should delegate repetitive, routine work. Preparation of recurring reports, maintaining leave and attendance records are some examples.
9. Good discipline is essential to good task performance. Discipline is reflected in the actions of employees on the job in the absence of supervision.
10. Disciplinary action may have to be taken when the positive aspects of discipline have failed. Reprimand, warning, and suspension are examples of disciplinary action.
11. If a situation calls for a reprimand, be sure it is deserved and remember it is to be done in private.

D. Dynamic Leadership
1. A style is a personal method or manner of exerting influence.
2. Authoritarian leaders often see themselves as the source of power and authority.
3. The democratic leader often perceives the group as the source of authority and power.
4. Supervisors tend to do better when using the pattern of leadership that is most natural for them.
5. Social scientists suggest that the effective supervisor use the leadership style that best fits the problem or circumstances involved.
6. All four styles—telling, selling, consulting, joining—have their place. Using one does not preclude using the other at another time.

7. The theory X point of view assumes that the average person dislikes work, will avoid it whenever possible, and must be coerced to achieve organizational objectives.
8. The theory Y point of view assumes that the average person considers work to be a natural as play, and, when the individual is committed, he requires little supervision or direction to accomplish desired objectives.
9. The leader's basic assumptions concerning human behavior and human nature affect his actions, decisions, and other managerial practices.
10. Dissatisfaction among employees is often present, but difficult to isolate. The supervisor should seek to weaken dissatisfaction by keeping promises, being sincere and considerate, keeping employees informed, and so forth.
11. Constructive suggestions should be encouraged during the natural progress of the work.

E. Processes for Solving Problems
1. People find their daily tasks more meaningful and satisfying when they can improve them.
2. The causes of problems, or the key factors, are often hidden in the background. Ability to solve problems often involves the ability to isolate them from their backgrounds. There is some substance to the cliché that some persons "can't see the forest for the trees."
3. New procedures are often developed from old ones. Problems should be broken down into manageable parts. New ideas can be adapted from old one.
4. People think differently in problem-solving situations. Using a logical, patterned approach is often useful. One approach found to be useful includes these steps:
   a. Define the problem
   b. Establish objectives
   c. Get the facts
   d. Weigh and decide
   e. Take action
   f. Evaluate action

F. Training for Results
1. Participants respond best when they feel training is important to them.
2. The supervisor has responsibility for the training and development of those who report to him.
3. When training is delegated to others, great care must be exercised to insure the trainer has knowledge, aptitude, and interest for his work as a trainer.
4. Training (learning) of some type goes on continually. The most successful supervisor makes certain the learning contributes in a productive manner to operational goals.
5. New employees are particularly susceptible to training. Older employees facing new job situations require specific training, as well as having need for development and growth opportunities.
6. Training needs require continuous monitoring.
7. The training officer of an agency is a professional with a responsibility to assist supervisors in solving training problems.

8. Many of the self-development steps important to the supervisor's own growth are equally important to the development of peers and subordinates. Knowledge of these is important when the supervisor consults with others on development and growth opportunities.

G. Health, Safety, and Accident Prevention
1. Management-minded supervisors take appropriate measures to assist employees in maintaining health and in assuring safe practices in the work environment.
2. Effective safety training and practices help to avoid injury and accidents.
3. Safety should be a management goal. All infractions of safety which are observed should be corrected without exception.
4. Employees' safety attitude, training and instruction, provision of safe tools and equipment, supervision, and leadership are considered highly important factors which contribute to safety and which can be influenced directly by supervisors.
5. When accidents do occur, they should be investigated promptly for very important reasons, including the fact that information which is gained can be used to prevent accidents in the future.

H. Equal Employment Opportunity
1. The supervisor should endeavor to treat all employees fairly, without regard to religion, race, sex, or national origin.
2. Groups tend to reflect the attitude of the leader. Prejudice can be detected even in very subtle form. Supervisors must strive to create a feeling of mutual respect and confidence in every employee.
3. Complete utilization of all human resources is a national goal. Equitable consideration should be accorded women in the work force, minority-group members, the physically and mentally handicapped, and the older employee. The important question is: "Who can do the job?"
4. Training opportunities, recognition for performance, overtime assignments, promotional opportunities, and all other personnel actions are to be handled on an equitable basis.

I. Improving Communications
1. Communications is achieving understanding between the sender and the receiver of a message. It also means sharing information—the creation of understanding.
2. Communication is basic to all human activity. Words are means of conveying meanings; however, real meanings are in people.
3. There are very practical differences in the effectiveness of one-way, impersonal, and two-way communications. Words spoken face-to-face are better understood. Telephone conversations are effective, but lack the rapport of person-to-person exchanges. The whole person communicates.
4. Cooperation and communication in an organization go hand in hand. When there is a mutual respect between people, spelling out rules and procedures for communicating is unnecessary.
5. There are several barriers to effective communications. These include failure to listen with respect and understanding, lack of skill in feedback, and misinterpreting the meanings of words used by the speaker. It is also common

practice to listen to what we want to hear, and tune out things we do not want to hear.
6. Communication is management's chief problem. The supervisor should accept the challenge to communicate more effectively and to improve interagency and intra-agency communications.
7. The supervisor may often plan for and conduct meetings. The planning phase is critical and may determine the success or the failure of a meeting.
8. Speaking before groups usually requires extra effort. Stage fright may never disappear completely, but it can be controlled.

J. Self-Development
1. Every employee is responsible for his own self-development.
2. Toastmaster and toastmistress clubs offer opportunities to improve skills in oral communications.
3. Planning for one's own self-development is of vital importance. Supervisors know their own strengths and limitations better than anyone else.
4. Many opportunities are open to aid the supervisor in his developmental efforts, including job assignments; training opportunities, both governmental and non-governmental—to include universities and professional conferences and seminars.
5. Programmed instruction offers a means of studying at one's own rate.
6. Where difficulties may arise from a supervisor's being away from his work for training, he may participate in televised home study or correspondence courses to meet his self-development needs.

K. Teaching and Training
1. The Teaching Process
Teaching is encouraging and guiding the learning activities of students toward established goals. In most cases this process consists of five steps: preparation, presentation, summarization, evaluation, and application.

   a. Preparation
   Preparation is two-fold in nature; that of the supervisor and the employee. Preparation by the supervisor is absolutely essential to success. He must know what, when, where, how, and whom he will teach. Some of the factors that should be considered are:
   1) The objectives
   2) The materials needed
   3) The methods to be used
   4) Employee participation
   5) Employee interest
   6) Training aids
   7) Evaluation
   8) Summarization

   Employee preparation consists in preparing the employee to receive the material. Probably the most important single factor in the preparation of the employee is arousing and maintaining his interest. He must know the objectives of the training, why he is there, how the material can be used, and its importance to him.

b. Presentation
In presentation, have a carefully designed plan and follow it. The plan should be accurate and complete, yet flexible enough to meet situations as they arise. The method of presentation will be determined by the particular situation and objectives.

c. Summary
A summary should be made at the end of every training unit and program. In addition, there may be internal summaries depending on the nature of the material being taught. The important thing is that the trainee must always be able to understand how each part of the new material relates to the whole.

d. Application
The supervisor must arrange work so the employee will be given a chance to apply new knowledge or skills while the material is still clear in his mind and interest is high. The trainee does not really know whether he has learned the material until he has been given a chance to apply it. If the material is not applied, it loses most of its value.

e. Evaluation
The purpose of all training is to promote learning. To determine whether the training has been a success or failure, the supervisor must evaluate this learning.
In the broadest sense, evaluation includes all the devices, methods, skills, and techniques used by the supervisor to keep himself and the employees informed as to their progress toward the objectives they are pursuing. The extent to which the employee has mastered the knowledge, skills, and abilities, or changed his attitudes, as determined by the program objectives, is the extent to which instruction has succeeded or failed.
Evaluation should not be confined to the end of the lesson, day, or program but should be used continuously. We shall note later the way this relates to the rest of the teaching process.

2. Teaching Methods
A teaching method is a pattern of identifiable student and instructor activity used in presenting training material.
All supervisors are faced with the problem of deciding which method should be used at a given time.

a. Lecture
The lecture is direct oral presentation of material by the supervisor. The present trend is to place less emphasis on the trainer's activity and more on that of the trainee.

b. Discussion
Teaching by discussion or conference involves using questions and other techniques to arouse interest and focus attention upon certain areas, and by doing so creating a learning situation. This can be one of the most

valuable methods because it gives the employees an opportunity to express their ideas and pool their knowledge.

c. Demonstration
The demonstration is used to teach how something works or how to do something. It can be used to show a principle or what the results of a series of actions will be. A well-staged demonstration is particularly effective because it shows proper methods of performance in a realistic manner.

d. Performance
Performance is one of the most fundamental of all learning techniques or teaching methods. The trainee may be able to tell how a specific operation should be performed but he cannot be sure he knows how to perform the operation until he has done so.
As with all methods, there are certain advantages and disadvantages to each method.

e. Which Method to Use
Moreover, there are other methods and techniques of teaching. It is difficult to use any method without other methods entering into it. In any learning situation, a combination of methods is usually more effective than any one method alone.

Finally, evaluation must be integrated into the other aspects of the teaching-learning process.

It must be used in the motivation of the trainees; it must be used to assist in developing understanding during the training; and it must be related to employee application of the results of training.

This is distinctly the role of the supervisor.

GLOSSARY OF BRIDGE ENGINEERING AND INSPECTION TERMS

	Page
Abutment ...... Aggregate	1
Allowable Unit Stress ...... Arch, Circular	2
Arch, Multi-Centered ...... Backstay	3
Backwall ...... Batter Pile	4
Bay ...... Berm	5
Blanket ...... Bracing	6
Bracing, (cont'd) ...... Brush Curb	7
Buckle ...... Cantilever Beam, Girder, or Truss	8
Cantilever Span ...... Check Analysis	9
Chord ...... Coefficient of Thermal Expansion	10
Cofferdam ...... Coping	11
Corbel ...... Covered Bridge	12
Cracking (reflection) ...... Curves in Plan and Profile	13
Cut ...... Diaphragm	14
Diaphragm Wall ...... Double Movable Bridge	15
Dowel ...... Drip Bead	16
Drip Hole ...... Expansion Dam	17
Expansion Joint ...... Falsework	18
Fascia ...... Fixed Bearing	19
Fixed Bridge ...... Foundation	20
Consolidated Soil Foundation ...... Girder Bridge	21
Girder Span ...... Guide Roller	22
Gusset ...... Hook Belt	23
Howe Truss ...... Joint	24
Keystone ...... Lateral Bracing	25
Lattice ...... Lock Device	26
Locking Mechanism ...... Pontoon Bridge	27
Retractile Draw Bridge ...... Overpass	28
Packing Ring ...... Pedestal Pier	29
Pile Pier or Bent ...... Pin Joint	30
Pin Packing ...... Priming Coat	31
Protection Fence ...... Reinforced Concrete Cantilever Wall	32
Rigid Frame Bridge ...... Rocker and Camshaft	33
Rolled Beams, Rolled Shapes ...... Sag Rod	34
Sash Brace ...... Shafts	35
Shear Lock ...... Skew Angle	36
Skewback ...... Span	37
Spandrel ...... Spreader	38
Springing Line ...... Stress	39
Stress (cont'd) ...... Sump	40
Superelevation ...... Sway Brace	41
Sway Frame ...... Toggle Joint	42
Tolerance ...... Truss	43
Truss Bridge ...... Warren Truss	44
Washer ...... Weep Hole	45
Weld ...... Wing Wall	46
Wing Wall (cont'd) ...... Working Stress	47

GLOSSARY OF BRIDGE ENGINEERING AND INSPECTION TERMS

A

Abutment. A substructure composed of stone, concrete, brick, or timber supporting the end of a single span or the extreme end of a multispan superstructure and, in general, retaining or supporting the approach embankment placed in contact therewith. (See also RETAINING WALLS, WING WALLS.)

The following types are now commonly used:

Cantilever Abutments. An abutment in which the stem or breast wall is fixed rigidly to the footing. The stem, acting as a cantilever beam transmits the horizontal earth pressure to the footing, which maintains stability by virtue of the dead weight of the abutment and of the soil mass resting on the rear portion, or heel, of the footing.

Cellular Abutment. An abutment in which the space between wings, breast wall, approach slab, and footings, instead of containing the approach fill, is hollow. This amounts to an R/C box or boxes comprising the abutment. On some bridges curtain walls are placed between the pier and abutment to simulate a cellular abutment.

Counterforted Abutment. An abutment which develops resistance to bending moment (or horizontal force) in the stem by use of counterforts. This permits the breast wall to be designed as a horizontal beam or slab spanning between counterforts, rather than as a vertical cantilever slab.

Gravity Abutment. A heavy abutment which resists the horizontal earth pressure by its own dead weight.

Integral Abutment. A small abutment cast monolithically with the end diaphragm of the deck. Although such abutments usually encase the ends of the deck beams and are pile supported, spread footings with a combination backwall and end diaphragm may also be used.

L-Abutment. A cantilever abutment with the stem flush with the toe of the footing, forming an L in cross section.

Spill-Thru Abutment. Consists essentially of two or more columns supporting a grade beam spanning the space between them. The approach embankment is retained only in part by the abutment since the embankment's sloped front and side portions extend with their normal slope to envelop the columns. Also called an arched abutment.

Shoulder Abutment. (*Full-Height Abutment.*) A cantilever abutment extending from the grade line of the road below to that of the road overhead. Usually set just off the shoulder.

Semi-Stub Abutment. Cantilever abutment founded part way up the slope, intermediate in size between a shoulder abutment and a stub abutment.

Straight Abutment. (*Trapezoidal or Block.*) An abutment whose stem and wings are in the same plane or whose stem is included within a length of retaining wall. In general, the stem wall is straight but will conform to the alignment of the retaining wall.

Stub Abutment. (*Perched Abutment, Dwarf Abutment.*) An abutment within the topmost portion of the end of an embankment or slope and, therefore, having a relatively small vertical height. While often engaging and supported upon piles driven through the underlying embankment or in-situ material, stubs may also be founded on gravel fill, the embankment, or natural ground itself.

Aggregate. The sand, gravel, broken stone, or combinations thereof with which the cementing material is mixed to form a mortar or concrete. The fine material used to produce mortar for stone and brick masonry and for the mortar component of concrete is commonly termed "fine aggregate" while the coarse material used in concrete only is termed "coarse aggregate."

Allowable Unit Stress. See STRESS.

Anchorage. The complete assemblage of members and parts whether composed of metal, masonry, wood or other material designed to hold in correct position the anchor span of a cantilever bridge, the end of a suspension span cable or a suspension span backstay; the end of a restrained beam, girder or truss span; a retaining wall, bulkhead, or other portion or part of a structure.

Anchor Span. The span which in conjunction with the uplift resisting anchorage device (if any) located at its outermost end, counterbalances and holds in equilibrium the fully cantilevered portion or arm extending in the opposite direction from the major point of support. See CANTILEVER BEAM, GIRDER, OR TRUSS.

Anchor Bolt. A bolt-like piece of metal commonly threaded and fitted with a nut, or a nut and washer at one end only, used to secure in a fixed position upon the substructure the end of a truss or girder, the base of a column, a pedestal, shoe, or other member of a structure. The end intended to engage the masonry may be formed in various ways depending somewhat upon the conditions attending its setting in final position. Among these are the following:

Hooked. Bent either cold or in a heated condition to form a hook-like anchorage. The hooked bolt is commonly built into the masonry preliminary to the placing of the member to be anchored and it may, therefore, be utilized to engage an anchor bar or other device imbedded in the masonry.

Ragged, Barbed or Fanged. Cut with a chisel to produce fin-like projections upon the surface.

Threaded. Shaped with a machine-cut thread. The thread anchorage is commonly supplemented by a nut, or a nut and anchor plate, when the bolt is to be built into the masonry instead of being set in a drilled hole.

Swedged. (*Notched, Hacked.*) Indented and bulged by swedging or nicked transversely and diagonally, or both, by cutting with a chisel.

Angle of Repose. (*Angle of Internal Friction.*) As applied to approach embankments or other earthwork construction: the batter or slope angle with the horizontal at which a given earth material will slide upon itself from a higher to a lower elevation. At all angles less than the angle of repose, the particles of earth are held in equilibrium by the forces of gravity and friction. Relatively slight variations in the quantity of contained moisture produce marked differences in the angle of repose. The inclined surface of a cut or of an embankment either naturally or artificially produced at the angle of repose is commonly described as being at "natural slope."

Anisotropy. The property of some engineering materials, such as wood, exhibiting different strengths in different directions.

Approach Slab. A heavy R/C slab placed on the approach roadway adjacent to and usually resting upon the abutment back wall. The function of the approach slab is to carry wheel loads on the approaches directly to the abutment, preventing the transfer of a horizontal dynamic force through the approach fill to the abutment stem.

Apron. A waterway bed protection consisting of timber, concrete, riprap, paving or other construction placed adjacent to substructure abutments and piers to prevent undermining by scour.

Arch. In general, any structure producing at its supports reactions having both vertical and horizontal components. However, this definition is not intended to include structures of the rigid frame type, although applicable thereto, but instead to apply only to those having throughout their length a curved shape, either actual or approximated.

Specific types of arches adapted to bridge construction derive their names either from the form of curve (or combination of curves assumed for the development of their intradosal surfaces), the support conditions, or their type of construction. The following constitute a portion of the types in use:

Elliptic Arch. One in which the intrados surface is a full half of the surface of an elliptical cylinder. This terminology is sometimes incorrectly applied to a multicentered arch. (An elliptic arch is fitted to stone masonry arches.)

Circular Arch. One in which the intrados surface is a portion of the surface of a right circular cylinder.

Multi-Centered Arch. One in which the intrados surface is outlined by two or more arcs having different radii by intersection tangentially and disposed symmetrically.

Open Spandrel Arch. An arch having spandrel walls with its spandrel unfilled. The arch ring receives its superimposed loads through these walls and, if necessary, through interior spandrel walls, tie or transverse walls, and/or interior columns.

A structure having the spandrel walls replaced by bays or panels with arches, lintel spans, or other constructions supporting the deck construction and these in turn supported by cross walls or columns resting upon the arch ring. See OPEN SPANDREL RIBBED ARCH.

Open Spandrel Ribbed Arch. A structure in which two or more comparatively narrow arch rings function in the place of an arch barrel. The ribs are rigidly secured in position by arch rib struts located at intervals along the length of the ring. The arch rings support a column type open spandrel construction sustaining the floor system and its loads.

Parabolic Arch. One in which the intrados surface is a segment of a symmetrical parabolic surface (suited to concrete arches).

Spandrel Arch. A stone or reinforced concrete arch span having spandrel walls to retain the spandrel fill or to support either entirely or in part the floor system of the structure when the spandrel is not filled.

Segmental Arch. An arch in which the intrados surface is less than half of the surface of a cylinder or cylindroid. Likewise it may take shape wherein any right section will show a parabolic curvature.

Two-Hinged Arch. An arch which is supported by a pinned connection at each support.

Three-Hinged Arch. An arch with end supports pinned and a third hinge (or pin) located somewhere near mid-span making the structure determinate.

Voussoir Arch. A hingeless arch with both supports fixed against rotation. Originally built of wedge-shaped stone blocks or voussoirs, the hingeless arch may also be built of concrete.

Arch Barrel. An arch ring that extends the width of the structure.

Arch Rib. An arch ring unit used in unfilled and open spandrel arch construction in reinforced concrete. Two or more relatively narrow arch ring units or sections support the columns of the bays or panels. The construction may involve a combination of arch ribs with spandrel walls providing an outward appearance akin to that of an unfilled spandrel arch.

One of the arched girders of a plate girder rib arch.

Arm. 1. The portion of a swing bridge or of a retractile draw bridge which forms the span or a portion of the span of the structure. 2. The rear or counterweight leaf of a bascule span. 3. The overhanging (or cantilever) portion of a cantilever bridge which supports the suspended span. 4. In statics, the perpendicular distance between the two parallel equal and opposite forces of a moment.

Armor. A secondary steel member installed to protect a vulnerable part of another member, e.g., steel angles placed over the edges of a joint.

Axle Load. The load borne by one axle of a traffic vehicle, a movable bridge, or other motive equipment or device and transmitted through a wheel or wheels to a supporting structure.

B

Back. See EXTRADOS.

Backfill. Material placed adjacent to an abutment, pier, retaining wall or other structure or part of a structure to fill the unoccupied portion of the foundation excavation.

Soil, usually granular, placed behind and within the abutment and wingwalls.

Backstay. The portion of the main suspension member of a suspension bridge extending between the tower and the anchorage. When this member continues over the towers from anchorage to anchorage, it does not support any portion of the bridge floor system which may be located between the tower and anchorage members of the structure.

A cable or chain attached at the top of a tower and extending to and secured upon the anchorage to resist overturning stresses exerted upon the tower by the suspension span attached to and located between towers.

Backwall. The topmost portion of an abutment above the elevation of the bridge seat, functioning primarily as a retaining wall with a live load surcharge. It may serve also as a support for the extreme end of the bridge deck and the approach slab.

Backwater. The water of a stream retained at an elevation above its normal level through the controlling effect of a condition existing at a downstream location such as a flood, an ice jam or other obstruction.

The increase in the elevation of the water surface above normal produced primarily by the stream width contraction beneath a bridge. The wave-like effect is most pronounced at and immediately upstream from an abutment or pier but extends downstream to a location beyond the body of the substructure part.

Balance Blocks. Blocks of cast iron, stone, concrete or other heavy weight material used to adjust the counterbalance of swing and lift spans.

Balance Wheel. (*Trailing Wheel.*) One of the wheels attached to the superstructure, normally having only a trailing contact upon a circular track surrounding the pivot of a center bearing swing bridge. These wheels maintain the proper balance and lateral stability of the superstructure by preventing excessive rocking or other motion due to wind pressures, shock from operating irregularities, or other causes. When correctly adjusted, a balance wheel will transmit only its own weight to the track and will revolve without load upon its axle.

Balancing Chain. See COUNTERBALANCING CHAIN.

Ballast. Filler material, usually broken stone or masonry, used either to stabilize a structure (as in filling a crib) or to transmit a vertical load to a lower level (as with a railroad track ballast).

Baluster. One of the column-like pieces composing the intermediate portion of a balustrade. Balusters may be varied in cross-sectional shape from round to square. See BALUSTRADE.

Balustrade. A railing composed of brick, stone or reinforced concrete located upon the retaining wall portion of an approach cut, embankment or causeway or at the outermost edge of the roadway or the sidewalk portion of a bridge to serve as a protection to vehicular and/or pedestrian traffic. Its major elements are: (1) plinth, (2) balusters, and (3) capping. However, the web portion may be built without openings instead of balustered or other open construction. See PARAPET.

Base Metal, Structure Metal, Parent Metal. The metal at and closely adjacent to the surface to be incorporated in a welded joint which will be fused, and by coalescence and interdiffusion with the weld will produce a welded joint.

Base Plate. A plate-shaped piece of steel, whether cast, rolled or forged, riveted upon or by other means made an integral part of the base portion of a column, pedestal or other member to transmit and distribute its load either directly or otherwise to the substructure or to another member.

Batten Plate. 1. A plate used to cover the joint formed by two abutting metal plates or shapes but ordinarily not considered as serving to transmit stress from one to the other. 2. A plate used in lieu of lacing to tie together the shapes comprising a built-up member. 3. A term sometimes used as synonymous with Stay Plates to indicate a plate in which the bar latticing or lacing of a bolted, riveted, or welded member terminates.

Batter. The inclination of a surface in relation to a horizontal or a vertical plane or occasionally in relation to an inclined plane. Batter is commonly designated upon bridge detail plans as so many inches to one foot. See RAKE.

Batter Pile. A pile driven in an inclined position to resist forces which act in other than a vertical direction. It may be computed to withstand these forces or, instead, may be used as a subsidiary part or portion of a structure to improve its general rigidity.

When driven and made fast upon the end of a pile bent or a piled pier located in a stream, river, or other waterway, it functions as a cutwater in dividing and deflecting floating ice and debris.

Bay. As applied to a stringer of multibeam structure, the area between adjacent stringers.

Bead. (*Run.*) A narrow continuous deposit of weld metal laid down in a single pass of fused filler metal.

Beam. 1. A simple or compound piece receiving and transmitting transverse or oblique stresses produced by externally applied loads, when supported at its end or at intermediate points and ends. The beam derives its strength from the development of internal bending or flexural stresses. 2. A rolled metal I-shaped or H-shaped piece. 3. An I-shaped piece or member composed of plates and angles or other structural shapes united by bolting, riveting or welding. In general, such pieces or members are described as built-up beams. These terms are applied to and define, in general terms only, variations in shape, size and arrangement of beam type members of reinforced concrete structures.

Reinforced Concrete Beam. Reinforced concrete beam is a construction wherein the tensile stresses, whether resulting from bending, shear, or combinations thereof produced by transverse loading, are by design carried by the metal reinforcement. The concrete takes compression (and some shear) only. It is commonly rectangular or Tee-shaped with its depth dimension greater than its stem width.

Reinforced Concrete T-Beam. Reinforced concrete T-beam derives its name from a similarity of shape to the letter "T," the head or topmost element of the letter consisting of a portion of the deck slab which is constructed integrally with the R/C beam stem.

Bearing Failure. Concerning the usual materials of construction, a crushing under extreme compressive load on an inadequate support; concerning soil, a shear failure in the supporting soil caused by excessively high pressures applied by a footing or pile.

Bearing. (*Fixed.*) A bearing which does not allow longitudinal movement.

Bearing Pad. A thin sheet of material placed between a masonry plate and the masonry bearing surface used to fill any voids due to imperfection of the masonry plate and bearing surface, to seal the interface, and to aid in even distribution of loads at the interface. The bearing pads may be made of alternating layers of red lead and canvas, of sheet lead, or of preformed fabric pads.

Bearing Seat. Top of masonry supporting bridge bearing.

Bearings. (*Live Load, Front Load, Outer.*) Live load bearings are a class of special bearings or supports installed on movable swing and bascule spans. These are engaged when the bridge is in the closed position taking the load off the trunnions and center pivot and preventing the outer end of the lift span from hammering on the rest pier under live load. Front load bearings are live load bearings placed on the support pier of a bascule bridge, and outer bearings are those on swing span and bascule rest piers.

Bed Rock. (*Ledge Rock.*) A natural mass formation of igneous, sedimentary, or metamorphic rock material either outcropping upon the surface, uncovered in a foundation excavation, or underlying an accumulation of unconsolidated earth material.

Bench Mark. A point of known elevation.

Bent. A supporting unit of a trestle or a viaduct type structure made up of two or more column or column-like members connected at their topmost ends by a cap, strut, or other member holding them in their correct positions. This connecting member is commonly designed to distribute the superimposed loads upon the bent, and when combined with a system of diagonal and horizontal bracing attached to the columns, the entire construction functions somewhat like a truss distributing its loads into the foundation.

When piles are used as the column elements, the entire construction is designated a "pile bent" or "piled bent" and, correspondingly, when those elements are framed, the assemblage is termed a "frame bent."

Berm. (*Berme.*) The line, whether straight or curved, which defines the location where the top surface of an approach embankment or causeway is intersected by the surface of the side slope. This term is synonymous with "Roadway Berm."

A horizontal bench located at the toe of slope of an approach cut, embankment or causeway to strengthen and secure its underlaying material against sliding or other displacement into an adjacent ditch, borrow pit, or other artificial or natural lower lying area.

Blanket. A protection against stream scour placed adjacent to abutments and piers and covering the stream bed for a distance from these structures considered adequate for the stream flow and stream bed conditions. The stream bed covering commonly consists of a deposit of stones of varying sizes which, in combination, will resist the scour forces. A second type consists of a timber framework so constructed that it can be ballasted and protected from displacement by being loaded with stones or with pieces of wrecked concrete structures or other adaptable ballasting material.

Boster. A block-like member composed of wood, metal, or concrete used to support a bearing on top of a pier cap or abutment bridge seat. It may adjust bearing heights and avoid constructing the bridge seat to the crown of the roadway, provide an area that may be ground to a precise elevation, or raise a bearing above moisture and debris that may collect on the bridge seat. See also BRIDGE PAD and BRIDGE SEAT PEDESTAL.

Bolted Joint. See RIVETED JOINT.

Bond. 1. In reinforced concrete, the grip of the concrete on the reinforcing bars, thereby preventing slippage of the bars. 2. The mechanical bond resulting from irregularities of surface produced in the manufacturing operations is an important factor in the strength of a reinforced concrete member. For plain round bar reinforcement, it is the difference between the force required to produce initial slip and the ultimate, producing failure. "Deformed" bars utilize this mechanical bond in conjunction with the surface bond. 3. The mechanical force developed between two concrete masses when one is cast against the already hardened surface of the other.

Bond Stress. A term commonly applied in reinforced concrete construction to the stress developed by the force tending to produce movement or slippage at the interface between the concrete and the metal reinforcement bars or other shapes.

Bowstring Truss. A general term applied to a truss of any type having a polygonal arrangement of its top chord members conforming to or nearly conforming to the arrangement required for a parabolic truss.

A truss having a top chord conforming to the arc of a circle or an ellipse. See PARABOLIC TRUSS.

Box Beam. A rectangular-shaped precast, and usually prestressed, concrete beam. These beams may be placed side by side, connected laterally, and used to form a bridge deck, with or without a cast-in-place slab or topping. In such cases, the beam units act together similar to a slab. Where a C-I-P slab is used and the units are spread, they act as beams.

Box Girder (concrete). A large concrete box-shaped beam, either reinforced or prestressed, usually multi-celled with several interior webs. The bottom slab of the girder serves as a flange only, while the top slab is both a flange and a transverse deck slab.

Box Girder (steel). A steel beam or girder, with a rectangular or trapezoidal cross section, composed of plates and angles or other structural shapes united by bolting, riveting, or welding, and having no interior construction except stiffeners, diaphragms, or other secondary bracing parts.

Recently, large steel multi-cell boxes with interior webs have been used as have composite steel box girders in which the concrete slab forms the top side of the box.

Bracing. A system of tension or of compression members, or a combination of these, forming with the part or parts to be supported or strengthened a truss or frame. It transfers wind, dynamic, impact, and vibratory stresses to the substructure and gives rigidity throughout the complete assemblage. In general, the bracing of a girder or of a truss span employs:

(1) A system of horizontal bracing in the planes of the top and bottom flanges or chords, designated according to its location, the top flange, top chord, top or overhead lateral brac-

ing, and the bottom flange, bottom chord or lower lateral bracing.

(2) Cross or X-bracing when placed transversely in vertical planes between beams and stringers and having diagonal members crossed, sometimes termed "Cross Frame." It functions as a diaphragm.

(3) Sway or buck bracing when placed transversely in vertical or nearly vertical planes between trusses. The term "overhead bracing," when applied here, is more appropriate than when applied to the top chord lateral bracing.

(4) Portal bracing consisting of a system of struts, ties and braces placed in the plane of the end posts of the trusses. Portal bracing may be in the plane of one flange of the end posts and described as a "single plane" portal or it may engage both flanges and be described as a "box portal." Without regard to its shape or details the entire portal bracing member is frequently designated as a "portal."

In general, the bracing of trestle and viaduct bents and towers employs:

(1) Transverse bracing engaging the columns of bents and towers in planes located either perpendicular or slightly inclined and transversely to the bridge alignment.

(2) Longitudinal bracing engaging the columns of bents and towers in planes located either perpendicular or slightly inclined and lengthwise with the bridge alignment.

(3) Horizontal bracing engaging the strut members of the transverse and longitudinal bracing of towers. Commonly this bracing is located in a horizontal position and is supported against sagging by vertical hangers or ties.

Bracket. A projecting support or brace-like construction fixed upon two intersecting members to function: (1) as a means of transferring reactions or shear stress from one to the other, or (2) to strengthen and render more rigid a joint connection of the members, or (3) to simply hold one member in a fixed position with relation to the other.

Breast Wall. (*Face Wall, Stem.*) The portion of an abutment between the wings and beneath the bridge seat. The breast wall supports the superstructure loads, and retains the approach fill.

Brick Veneer. See STONE FACING.

Bridge. A structure providing a means of transit for pedestrians and/or vehicles above the land and/or water surface of a valley, arroyo, gorge, river, stream, lake, canal, tidal inlet, gut or strait; above a road, highway, railway or other obstruction, whether natural or artificial.

In general, the essential parts of a bridge are: (1) the substructure consisting of its abutments and pier or piers supporting the superstructure, (2) the superstructure slab, girder, truss, arch or other span or spans supporting the roadway loads and transferring them to the substructure, and (3) the roadway and its incidental parts functioning to receive and transmit traffic loads.

Bridge (composite). A bridge whose concrete deck acts structurally with longitudinal main carrying members.

Bridge (indeterminate). A structure in which forces in the members cannot be determined by static equations alone.

Bridge (prestressed). A bridge whose main carrying members are made of prestressed concrete.

Bridge Pad. The raised, levelled area upon which the pedestal, shoe, sole, plate or other corresponding element of the superstructure takes bearing by contact. Also called Bridge Seat Bearing Area.

Bridge Seat. The top surface of an abutment or pier upon which the superstructure span is placed and supported. For an abutment it is the surface forming the support for the superstructure and from which the backwall rises. For a pier it is the entire top surface.

Bridge Site. The selected position or location of a bridge.

Bridging. A carpentry term applied to the cross-bracing, nailed or otherwise, fastened between wooden floor stringers, usually at the one-third span points, to increase the rigidity of the floor construction and to distribute more uniformly the live load and minimize the effects of impact and vibration.

Brush Curb. A narrow curb, 9 inches or less in width, which prevents a vehicle from brushing against the railing or parapet.

Buckle. To fail by an inelastic change in alignment (usually as a result of compression).

Buffer. (*Bumper.*) A mechanism designed to absorb the concussion or impact of a moving superstructure or other moving part when it swings, rises or falls to its limiting position of motion.

Built-Up Column. (*Built-Up Girder.*) A column, beam or girder, as the case may be, composed of plates and angles or other structural shapes united by bolting, riveting or welding to render the entire assemblage a unit. A built-up girder is commonly described as a plate girder.

Bulkhead. 1. A retaining wall-like structure commonly composed of driven piles supporting a wall or a barrier of wooden timbers or reinforced concrete members functioning as a constraining structure resisting the thrust of earth or of other material bearing against the assemblage. 2. A retaining wall-like structure composed of timber, steel, or reinforced concrete members commonly assembled to form a barrier held in a vertical or an inclined position by members interlocking therewith and extending into the restrained material to obtain the anchorage necessary to prevent both sliding and overturning of the entire assemblage.

Bumper. See BUFFER.

Buttress. A bracket-like wall, of full or partial height, projecting from another wall. The buttress strengthens and stiffens the wall against overturning forces applied to the opposite face by virtue of its depth in the direction of the loads. A buttress may be either integral with or independent of, but must be in contact with, the wall it is designed to reinforce. All parts of a buttress act in compression.

Buttressed Wall. See RETAINING WALL.

Butt Weld. A weld joining two abutting surfaces by depositing weld metal within an intervening space. This weld serves to unit the abutting surfaces of the elements of a member or to join members or their elements abutting upon or against each other.

C

Cable. One of the main suspension members of a suspension type bridge. Its function is to receive the bridge floor loads and transmit them to the towers and anchorages. See SUSPENSION BRIDGE.

Cable Band. The attachment device serving to fix a floor suspender upon the cable of a suspension bridge. In general this device consists of a steel casting provided with bolts or other appliances to securely seize it upon the cable and prevent the bank from slipping from its correct location.

Camber. The slightly arched form or convex curvature, provided in a single span or in a multiple span structure, to compensate for dead load deflection and to secure a more substantial and aesthetic appearance than is obtained when uniformly straight lines are produced. In general, a structure built with perfectly straight lines appears slightly sagged. This optical illusion is unsatisfactory and is most manifest in relatively long structures over rivers or other water areas.

The superelevation given to the extreme ends of a swing span during erection to diminish the deflection or "droop" of the arms when in open position-cantilevered from the center bearing. The decreased deformation below the normal position reduces the energy required to raise the ends in the closed position to permit the arms to function as simple spans.

Cantilever. A projecting beam, truss, or slab supported at one end only.

Cantilever Abutment. See ABUTMENT.

Cantilever Bridge. A general term applying to a bridge having a superstructure of the cantilever type.

Cantilever Beam, Girder, or Truss. A girder or truss having its members or parts so arranged that one or both of its end portions extend beyond the point or points of support. In general, it may have the following forms: (1) two projecting ends counterbalanced over a center support; (2) a projecting end counterbalanced in part by a portion extending beyond the point of support in the opposite direction, and having at its end an uplift resisting anchorage to complete the condition of equilibrium or, instead, the counterbalancing portion or anchor arm may in itself be adequate to counteract the projecting portion; (3) two projecting ends with an intermediate suspended portion, whose weight is completely counterbalanced by the anchor spans and/or anchorages. The end portions may or may not be alike in design.

Cantilever Span. A superstructure span of a cantilever bridge composed of two cantilever arms or of a suspended span connected with one or two cantilever arms.

Cap. (*Cap Beam, Cap Piece.*) The topmost piece or member of a viaduct, trestle, or frame bent serving to distribute the loads upon the columns and to hold them in their proper relative positions.

The topmost piece or member of a pile bent in a viaduct or trestle serving to distribute the loads upon the piles and to hold them in their proper relative positions. See PIER CAP and PILE CAP.

Capillary Action. The process by which water is drawn from a wet area to a dry area through the pores of a material.

Capstone. 1. The topmost stone of a masonry pillar, column or other structure requiring the use of a single capping element. 2. One of the stones used in the construction of a stone parapet to make up its topmost or "weather" course. Commonly this course projects on both the inside and outside beyond the general surface of the courses below it.

Carnegie Beam. See WIDE FLANGE.

Catch Basin. A receptacle, commonly box-shaped and fitted with a grilled inlet and a pipe outlet drain designed to collect the rain water and floating debris from the roadway surface and retain the solid material so that it may be removed at intervals. Catch basins are usually installed beneath the bridge floor or within the approach roadway with the grilled inlet adjacent to the roadway curb.

Catchment Area. See DRAINAGE AREA.

Catwalk. A narrow walkway for access to some part of a structure.

Cement Paste. The plastic combination of cement and water that supplies the cementing action in concrete.

Cement Matrix. The binding medium in a mortar or concrete produced by the hardening of the cement content of the mortar, concrete mixture of inert aggregates, or hydraulic cement and water.

Center Bearing. The complete assemblage of pedestal castings, pivot, discs, etc., functioning to support the entire dead load of a swing span when the end lifts are released or the span is revolving to "open" or to "closed position."

Center Discs. The assemblage of bronze, steel or other metal discs enclosed in the pivot of a center bearing swing span to reduce the frictional resistance in the operation of the span.

Center Lock. A locking device that transmits shear at the centerline of a double leaf bascule or double swing span bridge. This eliminates deflection and vibration at the center of the span.

Center Wedges. On a swing bridge, the assembly of pedestals and wedges located upon the pivot pier beneath the loading girder and operated mechanically to receive the pivot pier live loads and transmit them direct to the substructure, thus relieving the pivot casting from all, or nearly all, live load stress.

Centering. The supporting structure upon which the arch ring is constructed. This commonly consists of timber or metal framework having its topmost portion shaped to conform with the arch intrados and finished by covering with lagging or with bolsters, the latter being spaced to permit treatment of the mortared joints of stone masonry.

Support for formwork for any slab, beam, or other generally horizontal concrete structure.

Centering Device. The mechanical arrangement or device which guides the span of a bascule or a vertical lift span to its correct location upon its supports when being moved from open to closed position.

Channel Profile. Longitudinal section of a channel.

Chase. A channel, groove or elongated recess built into a structure surface for 1) the reception of a part forming a joint or (2) the installation of a member or part of the structure.

Check Analysis. See LADLE ANALYSIS.

Chord. In a truss, the upper and the lower longitudinal members, extending the full length and carrying the tensile and compressive forces which form the internal resisting moment, are termed chords. The upper portion is designated the upper, or top, chord and correspondingly the lower portion is designated the lower, or bottom, chord. The chords may be paralleled, or the upper one may be polygonal or curved (arched) and the lower one horizontal, or both may be polygonal. In general, the panel points of polygonal top chords are designed to follow the arc of a parabola and are, therefore, truly parabolic chords. Polygonal shaped chords are commonly described as "broken chords."

Chord Members. Trusses are commonly divided lengthwise into panels, the length of each being termed a panel length. The corresponding members of the chords are described as upper, or top, chord members and lower, or bottom, chord members.

Clearance. The unobstructed space provided: (1) in a through or half-through truss or a through plate girder type bridge, and (2) upon a deck truss or girder type bridge for the free passage of vehicular and pedestrian traffic. Clearance is measured in vertical and horizontal (lateral) dimensions and may or may not be determined or regulated by standard (clearance diagram) requirements. Vertical clearance for vehicles is measured above the elevation of the floor surface at its crown dimension while horizontal clearance is commonly measured from or with reference to the edge of travelway.

The unobstructed space provided below a bridge superstructure for (1) the passage of a river or stream with its surface burden of floating debris; (2) the passage of navigation craft commonly designated "clear headway" and (3) the passage of vehicular and pedestrian traffic. This form of clearance is frequently designated "under-clearance" to differentiate it from the provision for the requirements of the transportation service supported by the structure.

The space allowed for (1) the tolerance permitted in the dimensions of structural shapes; (2) the free assembling and adjustment of the elements of members or the members of a structure; and (3) the variations in dimensions incident to workmanship, temperature changes and minor irregularities. Among shop and field workers this condition is sometimes described as "the go and come" or "the play" allowance.

Clear Headway. (*Headway.*) The vertical clearance beneath a bridge structure available for the use of navigation. See CLEARANCE. In tidal waters headway is measured above mean high tide elevation.

Clear Span. The unobstructed space or distance between the substructure elements measured, by common practice, between faces of abutments and/or piers. However, when a structure is located upon a stream, river, tidal inlet or other waterway used by navigation, the clear span dimension is measured at mean low water elevation and may be the distance between guard or fender piers, dolphins or other constructions for the protection of navigation.

Clevis. A forked device used to connect the end of a rod upon a gusset plate or other structural part by means of a pin. It commonly consists of a forging having a forked end arranged to form two eyes or eyelets for engaging a pin and a nut-like portion, constructed integrally therewith, for engaging the correspondingly threaded end of a rod. However, the forked end (clevis) may form an integral portion of a rod without provision for adjustment of its length. An adjustable member having a fixed clevis at one end may be fitted with a thread and nut at its opposite end while one having fixed clevises at its ends may be fitted with either a sleeve nut or a turnbuckle in its midlength portion. Lateral bracing and tie-rod diagonals on old steel trusses often use clevises.

Clevis Bar. A member consisting of a rod having upset threaded ends fitted with clevises for engaging end connection pins. To render a clevis bar adjustable after assembling in a structure its ends are right and left threaded, or it may be constructed with a sleeve nut or a turnbuckle within its length, the end threads upon each of its sections being right and left hand and its clevises forged integrally with the body sections of the bar.

Clip Angle. See CONNECTION ANGLE.

Coefficient of Thermal Expansion. The unit strain produced in a material by a change of one degree in temperature.

Cofferdam. In general, an open box-like structure constructed to surround the area to be occupied by an abutment, pier, retaining wall or other structure and permit unwatering of the enclosure so that the excavation for the preparation of a foundation and the abutment, pier, or other construction may be effected in the open air. In its simplest form, the dam consists of interlocking steel sheet piles. See SHEET PILE COFFERDAM.

Collision Strut. A redundant member intended to reinforce the inclined end post of a through truss against damage from vehicular traffic. It joins the end post at a height above the roadway conceived to be the location of collision contact and, commonly, connects it with the first interior bottom chord panel point. The use of collision struts in highway bridges is limited.

Cold Work. The forming, such as rolling or bending, of a material at ordinary room temperature. Also applied to such deformation of steel elements in service under concentrated forces.

Column. A general term applying to a member resisting compressive stresses and having, in general, a considerable length in comparison with its transverse dimensions. This term is sometimes used synonymously for "post."

A member loaded primarily in compression. See also STRUT, POST, PILLAR.

Composite Joint. A joint in which the strength, rigidity or other requisites of its function are developed by combined mechanical devices, or by a fusion weld in conjunction with one or more mechanical means or appliances. The uncertain functioning of joints of this type makes their use undesirable.

Compound Roller. A roller consisting of a large solid cylinder at the center surrounded by a nest of smaller solid rollers having circular spacing bars engaging their ends and enveloped in a large hollow cylinder which forms the exterior surface of the assemblage. The large roller is commonly bored throughout its length at its center to permit observation of its interior material.

Compression (inelastic). Compression beyond the yield point.

Concrete. A composite material consisting essentially of a binding medium within which are embedded particles or fragments of a relatively inert mineral filler. In portland cement concrete, the binder or matrix, either in the plastic or the hardened state, is a combination of portland cement and water. The filler material, called aggregate, is generally graded in size from fine sand to pebbles or stones which may, in some concrete, be several inches in diameter.

Concrete is used in conjunction with stone fragments or boulders, of "one man" size or larger, imbedded therein to produce "cyclopean" or "rubble" concrete.

Connection Angle. (*Clip Angle.*) A piece or pieces of angle serving to connect two elements of a member or two members of a structure.

Consolidation. The time-dependent change in volume of a soil mass under compressive load caused by pore-water slowly escaping from the pores or voids of the soil. The soil skeleton is unable to support the load by itself and changes structure, reducing its volume and usually producing vertical settlements.

Continuous Girder. A general term applied to a beam or girder constructed continuously over one or more intermediate supports.

Continuous Spans. A beam, girder, or truss type superstructure designed to extend continuously over one or more intermediate supports.

Continuous Truss. A truss having its chord and web members arranged to continue uninterruptedly over one or more intermediate points of support, i.e., having three or more points of support.

Continuous Weld. A weld extending throughout the entire length of a joint.

Coping. A course of stone laid with a projection beyond the general surface of the masonry below it and forming the topmost portion of a retaining wall, pier, abutment, wingwall, etc. In general, the top surface is battered (washed) to prevent accumulation of rain or other moisture thereon.

A course of stone capping the curved or V-shaped extremity of a pier, providing a transition to the pier head proper. When so used it is commonly termed the "starling coping," "nose coping," the "cut-water coping" or the "pier extension coping."

In concrete construction the above terms are used without change.

Corbel. A piece or part constructed to project from the surface of a wall, column or other portion of a structure to serve as a support for a brace, short, beam or other member.

A projecting course or portion of masonry serving: (1) as a support for a superimposed member or members of a structure, or (2) as a part of the architectural treatment of a structure. In stone and brick masonry construction, this form of corbel is termed a "corbel course" implying greater length than that of a simple corbel.

Corrosion. The general disintegration and wasting of surface metal or other material through oxidation, decomposition, temperature, and other natural agencies.

Corrosion (electrolytic). Corrosion resulting from galvanic action.

Cotter Bolt. A bolt having a head at one end and near the opposite end a round hole or a hexagonal slot fitted with a cotter pin in the former or a tapered wedge in the latter. A cotter pin is usually formed by bending a piece of half-round rod to form a loop eye and a split body permitting its end to be splayed, thus holding it in position while a cotter wedge may be split for the same purpose, but either of these locking devices may be undivided and only bent sharply to prevent withdrawal. Cotter bolts are commonly fitted with one or two washers.

A cotter bolt fitted with a key is sometimes termed a "key bolt."

Counter. A truss web member which functions only when the span is partially loaded and shear stresses are opposite in sign to the normal conditions. The dead load of the truss does not stress the counter. See WEB MEMBERS.

Counterbalancing Chain. (*Balancing Chain*.) The chains made a part of the operating equipment of a vertical lift bridge to function as a weight counteracting the varying weight of the supporting cables incidental to the movements of the span.

Counterfort. A bracket-like wall projecting from another wall to which it adds stability by being integrally built with or otherwise securely attached to the side to which external forces are applied tending to overturn it. A counterfort, as opposed to a buttress, acts entirely to resist tensile and bending stresses. It may extend from the base either part or all the way to the top of the wall it is designed to reinforce.

Counterforted Wall. See RETAINING WALL.

Counterweight. A weight placed in position so as to counter balance the weight of a movable part (such as bascule leaf or vertical lift span).

Counterweight Well. (*Tail Pit*.) The enclosed space located beneath the bridge floor at the approach end to accommodate the counterweight and its supporting frame during the opening-closing cycle of the movable span of certain types of bascule bridge structures.

Course. In stone masonry, a layer of stone composed of either cut or uncut pieces laid with horizontal or slightly longitudinally inclined joints.

In brick masonry, a layer of bricks bedded in mortar.

Cover. In reinforced concrete, the clear thickness of concrete between a reinforcing bar and the surface of the concrete.

Cover Plate. A plate used in conjunction with flange angles or other structural shapes to provide additional flange section upon a girder, column, strut or similar member.

Covered Bridge. An indefinite term applied to a wooden bridge having in its construction a truss of any type adaptable to its location requirements. To prevent or delay deterioration of the timbers through infiltration of moisture into the framed or other joints, the entire structure, or instead, only its trusses are covered by a housing consisting of boards and shingles or other covering materials, fastened upon the side girts, rafters, purlins, or other parts intended to receive them. A covered bridge may be either a through or a deck structure. The former may be constructed with pony trusses.

Cracking (reflection). Visible cracks in an overlay indicating cracks in the concrete underneath.

Creep. An inelastic deformation that increases with time while the stress is constant.

Crib. A structure consisting of a foundation grillage combined with a superimposed framework providing compartments or coffers which are filled with gravel, stones, concrete or other material satisfactory for supporting the masonry or other structure to be placed thereon. The exterior portion may be planked or sheetpiled to protect the crib against damage by erosion or floating debris.

A structure consisting of a series of box-like compartments built of round or squared timbers having the crosstimbers (compartment division and end wall timbers) drift bolted and dove-tail framed or half framed to interlock with the side timbers, thus producing a rigid framework of the height desired. A portion of the compartment is constructed with floors to serve as ballast boxes for loading and sinking the crib in its final position after which the remaining compartments are filled or partially filled with gravel, stones or other material to render the entire structure stable against the forces to which it may be subjected.

This latter type of crib is used as a protection against wave action and stream currents producing scour and erosion adjacent to bridge structures to prevent undermining of abutments and piers or other substructure elements and also to serve as a training wall averting changes in shore and bank locations.

Cribbing. A construction consisting of wooden, metal or reinforced concrete units so assembled as to form an open cellular-like structure for supporting a superimposed load or for resisting horizontal or overturning forces acting against it.

Cross Frames. Transverse bracings between two main longitudinal members. See DIAPHRAGM and BRACING.

Cross Girder, Transverse Girder. A term applied to large timber members and to metal and reinforced concrete girder-like members placed generally perpendicular to and connected upon the main girders or trusses of a bridge span, including intermediate and end floor beams.

Cross Wall. See DIAPHRAGM WALL.

Crown of Roadway. 1. The crest line of the convexed surface. 2. The vertical dimension describing the total amount the surface is convexed or raised from gutter to crest. This is sometimes termed the cross fall of roadway.

Culvert. A small bridge constructed entirely below the elevation of the roadway surface and having no part or portion integral therewith. Structures over 20 feet in span parallel to the roadway are usually called bridges, rather than culverts; and structures less than 20 feet in span are called culverts even though they support traffic loads directly.

Curb. A stone, concrete or wooden barrier paralleling the side limit of the roadway to guide the movement of vehicle wheels and safeguard bridge trusses, railings or other constructions existing outside the roadway limit and also pedestrian traffic upon sidewalks from collision with vehicles and their loads.

Curb Inlet. See SCUPPER.

Curtain Wall. A term commonly applied to a thin masonry wall not designed to support superimposed loads either vertically or transversely.

A thin vertically placed and integrally built portion of the paving slab of a culvert intended to protect the culvert against undermining by stream scour. A similar construction placed in an inclined position is termed an "apron wall" or "apron."

A wall uniting the pillar or shaft portions of a dumbbell pier. However, its service function is that of a frame composed of struts and braces rendering the entire structure integral in its action. As here applied the term is synonymous with "diaphragm wall."

Curve Banking. See SUPERELEVATION.

Curves in Plan and Profile. A roadway may be curved in its lateral alignment, its vertical contour, or in both alignment and contour combined. The primary curves are described as:

1. Horizontal Curve. A curve in the plan location defining the alignment.

2. Vertical Curve. A curve in the profile location defining the elevation.

Cut. (*Cutting.*) That portion of a highway, railway, canal, ditch or other artificial construction of similar character produced by the removal of the natural formation of earth or rock whether sloped or level. The general terms "side hill cut" and "through cut" are used to describe the resulting cross sections of the excavations commonly encountered.

Cut Slope. A term applied to the inclined surface of an approach cut terminating in the ditch or gutter at its base, which in turn serves to remove accumulations of water from all areas drained into it.

Cylinder Pier. See PIER.

D

Dead Load. A static load due to the weight of the structure itself.

Dead Man. A general term applied to an anchorage member engaging the end of a stay rod, cable or other tie-like piece or part. The anchorage member is made secure through the resistance to movement produced by the earth, stone, brickbats, or other material used to embed and cover the anchor piece which may consist of a wooden log or timber, a metal beam or other structural shape, a quarried stone boulder or any other adaptable object. This type of anchor member is used to restrain and hold in position piles, bulkheads, cribs, and other constructions against horizontal movement as well as to resist the stresses of tie members acting in inclined and vertical directions.

Debris Rack. A grill type barrier used to intercept debris above a sewer or culvert inlet.

Deck. That portion of a bridge which provides direct support for vehicular and pedestrian traffic. The deck may be either a reinforced concrete slab, timber flooring, a steel plate or grating, or the top surface of abutting concrete members or units. While normally distributing load to a system of beams and stringers, a deck may also be the main supporting element of a bridge, as with a reinforced concrete slab structure or a laminated timber bridge.

Deck Bridge. A bridge having its floor elevation at, nearly at, or above the elevation of the uppermost portion of the superstructure.

Decking. A term specifically applied to bridges having wooden floors and used to designate the flooring only. It does not include the floor stringers, floor beams, or other members serving to support the flooring.

Deformation (elastic). Deformation occurring when stress in a material is less than the yield point. If the stress is removed, the material will return to its original shape.

Depth of Truss. As applied to trusses having parallel chords and to polygonal trusses having a midspan length with parallel chords; the vertical distance between the centerlines of action of the top and bottom chords.

Design Load. The loading comprising magnitudes and distributions of wheel, axle or other concentrations used in the determination of the stresses, stress distributions and ultimately the cross-sectional areas and compositions of the various portions of a bridge structure.

The design loading or loadings fixed by a specification are very commonly composite rather than actual, but are predicated upon a study of various types of vehicles. In lieu of a loading so determined for use as "standard," an equivalent uniform load designed to produce resulting structures practically identical with those evolved by the use of such loadings may be used. One or more concentrated loads may be used in conjunction with the uniform load to secure the effect corresponding to the incorporation of especially heavy vehicles within the normally maximum traffic considered as likely to pass upon a given bridge or a series of bridges. Such equivalent loadings are merely a convenience facilitating design operations.

In rating bridges for the Bridge Inspection Manual, either the H or HS trucks with their alternate lane loadings may be used. Or, if desired, the special legal limit trucks: Type 3, Type 3S 2, and Type 3–3, may be used.

Diagonal. See WEB MEMBERS.

Diagonal Stay. A cable support in a suspension bridge extending diagonally from the tower to the roadway system to add stiffness to the structure and diminish the deformations and undulations resulting from traffic service.

Diaphragm. A reinforcing plate or member placed within a member or deck system, respectively, to distribute stresses and improve strength and rigidity. See BRACING.

Diaphragm Wall (cross wall). A wall built transversely to the longitudinal centerline of a spandrel arch serving to tie together and reinforce the spandrel walls together with providing a support for the floor system in conjunction with the spandrel walls. To provide means for the making of inspections the diaphragms of an arch span may be provided with manholes.

The division walls of a reinforced concrete caisson dividing its interior space into compartments and reinforcing its walls. A wall serving to subdivide a box-like structure or portion of a structure into two or more compartments, or sections.

Dike. (*Dyke*). An earthen embankment constructed to provide a barrier to the inundation of an adjacent area which it encloses entirely or in part.

When used in conjunction with a bridge, its functions are commonly those of preventing stream erosion and localized scour and/or to so direct the stream current that debris will not accumulate upon bottom land adjacent to approach embankments, abutments, piers, towers, or other portions of the structure.

This term is occasionally misapplied to crib construction used to accomplish a like result. See CRIB.

Spur Dike. A projecting jetty-like construction placed adjacent to an abutment of the "U," "T," block or arched type upon the upstream and downstream sides, but sometimes only on the upstream side, to secure a gradual contraction of the stream width and induce a free even flow of water adjacent to and beneath a bridge. They may be constructed in extension of the wing wall or a winged abutment.

The common types of construction used for water wings are: (1) Wooden cribs filled with stones; (2) embankments riprapped on the waterway side; and (3) wooden and metal sheet piling.

Spur dikes serve to prevent stream scour and undermining of the abutment foundation and to relieve the condition which otherwise would tend to gather and hold accumulations of stream debris against and adjacent to the upstream side of the abutment.

Dimension Stone. A stone of relatively large dimensions, the face surface of which is either chisel or margin drafted but otherwise rough and irregular, commonly called either "rock face" or "quarry face."

Stones quarried with the dimensions large enough to provide cut stones with given finished dimensions.

Distribution Girder. A beam or girder-like member forming a part of the frame by which the dead and live loads are transmitted to the drum girder of a rim-boaring swing span.

Ditch. See DRAIN.

Diversion Drain. (*Diversion Flume.*) An open top paved drain constructed for the purpose of diverting and conveying water from a roadway gutter down the inclined surface of a bridge approach embankment or causeway.

Dolphin. A group or cluster of piles driven in one to two circles about a center pile and drawn together at their top ends around the center pile to form a buffer or guard for the protection of channel span piers or other portions of a bridge exposed to possible injury by collision with waterbound traffic. The tops of the piles are served with a wrapping consisting of several plies of wire, rope, coil, twist link, or stud link anchor chain, which, by being fastened at its ends only, renders itself taut by the adjustments of the piles resulting from service contact with ships, barges, or other craft. The center pile may project above the others to serve as a bollard for restraining and guiding the movements of water-borne traffic units.

Single steel and concrete piles of large size may also be used as dolphins.

Double Movable Bridge. A bridge in which the clear span for navigation is produced by joining the arms of two adjacent swing spans or the leaves of two adjacent bascule spans at or near the center of the navigable channel. The arms or leaves may act as cantilevers with a shear lock at their junction to provide for the passage of traffic over the joint. The leaves of bascules may be equipped to act as a hinged arch. Spans comprised of two bascule leaves are called double leaf bascule bridges. See MOVABLE BRIDGE.

Dowel. A short length of metal bar, either round or square, used to attach and prevent movement and displacement of wooden, stone, concrete, or metal pieces when placed in a bored, drilled, or cored hole located in their contact surfaces. A dowel may or may not be sized to provide a driving fit in the hole. In stone and premolded concrete structures the dowels are commonly set in lead, mortar, or other material filling the portions of the holes not occupied by the dowels. In concrete construction the plastic concrete is usually either placed around a dowel or the dowel is thrust into it.

In general, dowels function to resist shear forces, although footing dowels in reinforced concrete walls and columns resist bending forces.

Drain. (*Ditch, Gutter.*) A trench or trough-like excavation made to collect water. In general a drain is considered as functioning to collect and convey water whereas a ditch may only serve to collect it.

A gutter is a paved drain commonly constructed in conjunction with the curbs of the roadway or instead built closely adjacent to the paved portion of the roadway.

Drain Hole. (*Drip Hole.*) An aperture extending through a wall to provide an egress for water which might otherwise accumulate upon one of its sides. In this connection the term "weep hole" and "drain hole" are commonly used. See WEEP HOLE.

A cored, punched or bored hole in a box or trough shaped member or part to provide means for the egress of accumulated water or other liquid matter. In areas exposed to freezing temperatures, these holes are used to prevent damage by the expansive force incident to the freezing of water accumulations.

Drainage. The interception and removal of water from the roadway and/or sidewalk surfaces of a bridge or its approaches; from beneath the paved or otherwise prepared roadway and/or sidewalk surfaces of the approaches and from the sloped surfaces of hillsides, cuts, embankments, and causeways; from the backfill or other material in contact with abutments, retaining walls, counterweight wells or parts of a bridge or incidental structure.

A ditch, drain, gutter, gully, flume, catch basin, downspout, scupper, weep hole, or other construction or appliance facilitating the interception and removal of water.

Drainage Area, Catchment Area. The area from which the run-off water passing beneath a bridge or passing a specific location in a river or stream is produced.

Drawbridge. A general term applied to a bridge over a navigable stream, river, lake, canal, tidal inlet, gut or strait having a movable superstructure span of any type permitting the channel to be freed of its obstruction to navigation. A popular but imprecise term.

Probably the earliest use of a drawbridge was for military purposes, utilizing a single leaf hinged frame lifted up or let down by a comparatively simple manually operated mechanism.

Draw Rest. A support constructed upon a fender or guard pier and equipped with a latch block for holding a swing span in open position. This support may consist of a block of masonry, a rigid metal frame or other construction adapted to the service requirements.

Draw Span. A general term applied to either a swing or a retractile type movable superstructure span of a bridge over a navigable stream, river, lake, canal, tidal inlet, gut or strait. See MOVABLE BRIDGE.

Drift Bolt. A short length of metal bar, either round or square, used to connect and hold in position wooden members placed in contact. It may or may not be made with a head and a tapered point. Drift bolts are commonly driven in holes having a diameter slightly less than the bolts. This condition appears to be the recognized practical difference between a drift bolt and a dowel. The difference is more a matter of usage of terms rather than of functions to be performed.

Drip Bead. A channel or groove in the under side of a belt course, coping, or other protruding exposed portion of a masonry structure intended to arrest the downward flow of rain water and cause it to drip off free from contact with surfaces below the projection.

Drip Hole. See DRAIN HOLE.

Drop Inlet. A box-like construction commonly built integrally with the upstream end of a culvert with provision for the water to flow in at its top and to enter the culvert proper at its bottom or within its bottom portion. Vegetable or other material likely to become lodged in the culvert may be retained in the base portion of this receiving device by constructing its base to form a sump below the inlet elevation of the culvert. The culvert inlet may or may not be provided with a grating.

Drum Girder. (*Rim Girder.*) The circular plate girder forming a part of a swing bridge turntable transferring its loadings to the rollers and to the circular track upon which they travel. When the swing span is in "closed" position the drum girder track receives the superstructure dead and live loads and transmits these to the substructure bearing area beneath the track.

Ductility. The ability to withstand non-elastic deformation without rupture.

Dyke. See DIKE.

E

Efflorescence. A white deposit on concrete or brick caused by crystallization of soluble salts brought to the surface by moisture in the masonry.

Elastic Deformation. See DEFORMATION.

Elastomer. A natural or synthetic rubber-like material.

Electrolytic Corrosion. See CORROSION (ELECTROLYTIC).

Element. Metal Structures. An angle, beam, plate or other rolled, forged or cast piece of metal forming a part of a built piece. For Wooden Structures. A board, plank, joist, scantling or other fabricated piece forming a part of a built piece.

End Block. On a prestressed concrete beam, the thickening of the web or increase in beam width at the end to provide adequate anchorage bearing for the post-tensioning wires, rods, or strands.

End Hammer. The hammering action of an end lift device upon its pedestal or bearing plate resulting from the deflections and vibrations set up by the movements of traffic upon a swing span when the lifting device is improperly adjusted.

End Lift. The mechanism consisting of wedges, toggles, link-and-roller, rocker-and-eccentric or other devices combined with shafts, gears, or other operating parts requisite to remove the camber or "droop" of a swing span.

End Post. The end compression member of a truss, either vertical or inclined in position and extending from chord to chord, functioning to transmit the truss end shear to its end bearing.

Epoxy. A synthetic resin which cures or hardens by chemical reaction between components which are mixed together shortly before use.

Equalizer. A balance lever engaging the counterweight and the suspending cables of a vertical lift span as a means of adjustment and equalization of the stresses in the latter.

Equilibrium. In statics, the condition in which the forces acting upon a body are such that no external effect (or movement) is produced.

Equivalent Uniform Load. A load having a constant intensity per unit of its length producing an effect equal or practically equal to that of a live load consisting of vehicle axle or wheel concentrations spaced at varying distances apart, when used as a substitute for the latter in determining the stresses in a structure.

Expansion Bearing. A general term applied to a device or assemblage designed to transmit a reaction from one member or part of a structure to another and to permit the longitudinal movements resulting from temperature changes and superimposed loads without transmitting a horizontal force to the substructure.

The expansion bearing is designed to permit movement by overcoming sliding, rolling or other friction conditions. In general, provision is made for a movement equal to 1¼" in 100', thus providing for ordinary irregularities in field erection and adjustment.

Expansion Dam. The part of an expansion joint serving as an end form for the placing of concrete at a joint. Also applied to the expansion joint device itself.

Expansion Joint. A joint designed to provide means for expansion and contraction movements produced by temperature changes, loadings or other agencies.

Expansion Rocker. An articulated assemblage forming a part of the movable end of a girder or truss and facilitating the longitudinal movements resulting from temperature changes and superimposed loads. Apart from its hinge connection the rocker proper is a cast or built-up member consisting essentially of a circular segment integrally joined by a web-like portion to a hub fitted for hinge action either with a pin hole or by having its ends formed into trunnions. In its service operation the rocker is commonly supported upon a shoe plate or pedestal. Strictly speaking, this is a segment of a roller. A short cast or built-up member hinged at both ends, or instead hinged at one end and provided with a circular segment or spherical type bearing at the other to facilitate expansion and contraction on other longitudinal rotational movements.

Expansion Roller. A cylinder so mounted that by revolution it facilitates expansion, contraction or other movements resulting from temperature changes, loadings or other agencies.

Expansion Shoe. (*Expansion Pedestal.*) An expansion bearing member or assemblage designed to provide means for expansion and contraction or other longitudinal movements. In general, the term "shoe" is applied to an assemblage of structural plates or plate-like castings permitting movement by sliding while the term "pedestal" is used to describe assemblages of castings or built-up members securing a somewhat greater total depth and providing for movement either by sliding or by rolling.

The masonry plate or casting is commonly held in a fixed position by anchor bolts and the superimposed shoe plate or pedestal is free to move longitudinally upon it or upon intervening rollers but is restrained from transverse movement either by a rib and slot, by pintles, by anchorage or by anchorage in combination with one of the first two mentioned. The term "bed plate" is sometimes used to designate the bottom portion of the assemblage.

Extrados. (*Back.*) 1. The curved surface of an arch farthest from its longitudinal construction axis or axes. 2. The curve defining the exterior surface of an arch.

Eyebar. A member consisting of a rectangular bar body with enlarged forged ends or heads having holes through them for engaging connecting pins.

An adjustable eyebar is composed of two sections fitted with upset threaded ends engaging a sleevenut or a turnbuckle.

Eyebolt. (*Ringbolt.*) A bolt having a forged eye at one end used, when installed in a structure, to provide means for making fast the end of a cable, a hooked rod or other part or portion of the bridge, or instead to provide a means of anchorage for unrelated equipment or structures.

A ringbolt is essentially an eyebolt fitted with a ring to serve the same purpose as described above for an eyebolt with added articulation.

F

Face Stones. The stones exposed to view in the face surfaces of abutments, piers, arches, retaining walls or other stone structures.

Face Wall.

    Abutment. See BREAST WALL.

    Spandrel Arch Structure. The outermost spandrel walls providing the face surfaces of the completed structure. See SPANDREL ARCH.

Factor of Safety. A factor or allowance predicated by common engineering practice upon the failure stress or stresses assumed to exist in a structure or a member or part thereof. Its purpose is to provide a margin in the strength, rigidity, deformation and endurance of a structure or its component parts compensating for irregularities existing in structural materials and workmanship, uncertainties involved in mathematical analysis and stress distribution, service deterioration and other unevaluated conditions.

Falsework. A temporary wooden or metal framework built to support without appreciable settlement and deformation the weight of a structure during the period of its construction and until it becomes self-supporting. In general, the arrangement of its details are devised to facilitate the construction operations and provide for economical removal and the salvaging of material suitable for reuse.

Fascia. An outside, covering member designed on the basis of architectural effect rather than strength and rigidity although its function may involve both.

A light, stringer-like member spanning longitudinally between cantilever brackets which support large overhangs on girder or beam bridges.

Fascia Girder. As exposed outermost girder of a span sometimes treated architecturally or otherwise to provide an attractive appearance.

Fatigue. The tendency of a member to fail at a lower stress when subjected to cyclical loading than when subjected to static loading.

Felloe Guard. See WHEEL GUARD.

Fender. 1. A structure placed at an upstream location adjacent to a pier to protect it from the striking force, impact and shock of floating stream debris, ice floes, etc. This structure is sometimes termed an "ice guard" in latitudes productive of lake and river ice to form ice flows. 2. A structure commonly consisting of dolphins, capped and braced rows of piles or of wooden cribs either entirely or partially filled with rock ballast, constructed upstream and downstream from the center and end piers (or abutments) of a fixed or movable superstructure span to fend off water-borne traffic from collision with these substructure parts, and in the case of a swing span, with the span while in its open position.

Fender Pier. A pier-like structure which performs the same service as a fender but is generally more substantially built. These structures may be constructed entirely or in part of stone or concrete masonry. See GUARD PIER.

Field Coat. A coat of paint applied upon the priming or base coat or upon a coat subsequently applied and, generally, after the structure is assembled and its joints completely connected by bolts, rivets or welds. This application is quite commonly a part of the field erection procedure and is, therefore, termed field painting.

Fill. (*Filling.*) Material, usually earth, used for the purpose of raising or changing the surface contour of an area, or for constructing an embankment.

Filler (Filler Plate). In wooden and structural steel construction. A piece used primarily to fill a space beneath a batten, splice plate, gusset, connection angle, stiffener or other element.

Filler Metal. Metal prepared in wire, rod, electrode or other adaptable form to be fused with the structure metal in the formation of a weld.

Filler Plate. See FILLER.

Fillet. 1. A curved portion forming a junction of two surfaces which would otherwise intersect at an angle. 2. In metal castings and rolled structural shapes a fillet is used to disseminate and relieve the shrinkage or other stresses tending to overstress and, perhaps, rupture the junction material. In castings it may also provide means for movement to take place at locations where the rigidity of the mold would otherwise resist and obstruct this action. 3. In concrete construction the use of mitered fillets in internal corners of forms not only serves the purposes applying to castings but also facilitates both the placing of concrete and the subsequent removal of forms.

Fillet Weld. A weld joining intersecting members by depositing weld metal to form a near-triangular or fillet shaped junction of the surfaces of the members so joined. This weld serves to unite the intersecting surfaces of two elements of a member.

Filling. See FILL.

Finger Dam. Expansion joint in which the opening is spanned by meshing steel fingers or teeth.

Fish Belly. A term applied to a girder or a truss having its bottom flange or its bottom chord, as the case may be, constructed either haunched or bow-shaped with the convexity downward. See LENTICULAR TRUSS.

Fixed-Ended Arch. See VOUSSOIR ARCH.

Fixed Bearing. The plates, pedestals, or other devices designed to receive and transmit to the substructure or to another supporting member or structure the reaction stresses of a beam, slab, girder, truss, arch or other type of superstructure span.

The fixed bearing is considered as holding the so-termed "fixed end" of the structure rigidly in position, but in practice the clearance space commonly provided in the anchorage may permit a relatively small amount of movement.

Fixed Bridge. A bridge having its superstructure spans fixed in position except that provision may be made in their construction for expansion and contraction movements resulting from temperature changes, loadings, or other agencies.

Fixed Span. A superstructure span having its position practically immovable, as compared to a movable span.

Flange. The part of a rolled I-shaped beam or of a built-up girder extending transversely across the top and bottom edges of the web. The flanges are considered to carry the compressive and tensile forces that comprise the internal resisting moment of the beam, and may consist of angles, plates, or both.

Flange Angle. An angle used to form a flange element of a built-up girder, column, strut or similar member.

Floating Bridge. In general this term means the same as "Pontoon Bridge." However, its parts providing buoyancy and supporting power may consist of logs or squared timbers, held in position by lashing pieces, chains or ropes, and floored over with planks, or the bridge itself may be of hollow cellular construction.

Floating Foundation. A term sometimes applied to a "foundation raft" or "foundation grillage." Used to describe a soil-supported raft or mat foundation with low bearing pressures.

Flood Gate. (*Tide Gate.*) An automatically operated gate installed in a culvert or bridge waterway to prevent the ingress of flood or tide water to the area drained by the structure.

Floor. See DECK.

Floor Beam. A beam or girder located transversely to the general alignment of the bridge and having its ends framed upon the columns of bents and towers or upon the trusses or girders of superstructure spans. A floor beam at the extreme end of a girder or truss span is commonly termed an end floor beam.

Floor System. The complete framework of floor beams and stringers or other members supporting the bridge floor proper and the traffic loading including impact thereon.

Flow Line. The surface of a water course.

Flux. A material which prevents, dissolves, and removes oxides from metal during the welding process. It may be in the coating on a metal stick electrode or a granular mass covering the arc in submerged arc welding and protects the weld from oxidation during the fusion process.

Footbridge. (*Pedestrian Bridge.*) A bridge designed and constructed to provide means of traverse for pedestrian traffic only.

Footing. (*Footing Course, Plinth.*) The enlarged, or spread-out, lower portion of a substructure, which distributes the structure load either to the earth or to supporting piles. The most common footing is the concrete slab, although stone piers also utilize footings. Plinth refers to stone work as a rule. "Footer" is a local term for footing.

Foot Wall. See TOE WALL.

Forms. (*Form Work, Lagging, Shuttering.*) The constructions, either wooden or metal, providing means for receiving, molding and sustaining in position the plastic mass of concrete placed therein to the dimensions, outlines and details of surfaces planned for its integral parts throughout its period of induration or hardening.

The terms "forms" and "form work" are synonymous. The term "lagging" is commonly applied to the surface shaping areas of forms producing the intradoses of arches or other curved surfaces, especially when strips are used.

Forms. (SIP, Stay-in-Place.) A prefabricated metal concrete deck form that will remain in place after the concrete has set.

Form Work. See FORMS.

Foundation. The supporting material upon which the substructure portion of a bridge is placed. A foundation is "natural" when consisting of natural earth, rock or near-rock material having stability adequate to support the superimposed loads without lateral displacement or compaction entailing appreciable settlement or

deformation. Also, applied in an imprecise fashion to a substructure unit.

Consolidated Soil Foundation. A foundation of soft soil rendered more resistant to its loads by (1) consolidating the natural material, (2) by the incorporation of other soil material (sand, gravel, etc.) into the soft material, and (3) by the injection of cementing materials into the soil mass which will produce consolidation by lapidification.

Pile or Piled Foundation. A foundation reinforced by driving piles in sufficient number and to a depth adequate to develop the bearing power required to support the foundation load.

Foundation Excavation. (*Foundation Pit.*) The excavation made to accommodate a foundation for a retaining wall, abutment, pier or other structure or element thereof.

Foundation Grillage. A construction consisting of steel, timber, or concrete members placed in layers. Each layer is normal to those above and below it and the members within a layer are generally parallel, producing a crib or grid-like effect. Grillages are usually placed under very heavy concentrated loads.

Foundation Load. The load resulting from traffic, superstructure, substructure, approach embankment, approach causeway, or other incidental load increment imposed upon a given foundation area.

Foundation Pile. A pile, whether of wood, reinforced concrete, or metal used to reinforce a foundation and render it satisfactory for the supporting of superimposed loads.

Foundation Pit. See FOUNDATION EXCAVATION.

Foundation Seal. A mass of concrete placed underwater within a cofferdam for the base portion of an abutment, pier, retaining wall or other structure to close or seal the cofferdam against incoming water from foundation springs, fissures, joints or other water carrying channels. See TREMIE.

Foundation Stone. The stone or one of the stones of a course having contact with the foundation of a structure.

Frame. A structure having its parts or members so arranged and secured that the entire assemblage may not be distorted when supporting the loads, forces, and physical pressures considered in its design. The framing of a truss relates to the design and fabrication of the joint assemblages.

Framing. The arrangement and manner of joining the component members of a bent, tower, truss, floor system or other portion of a bridge structure to insure a condition wherein each element and member may function in accord with the conditions attending its design. Framing must be interpreted as including both design and fabrication for the complete structure.

Friction Roller. A roller placed between parts or members intended to facilitate change in their relative positions by reducing the frictional resistance to translation movement.

Frost Heave. The upward movement of and force exerted by soil due to alternate freezing and thawing of retained moisture.

Frost Line. The depth to which soil may be frozen.

G

Galvanic Action. Electrical current between two unlike metals.

Gauge. The distance between parallel lines of rails, rivet holes, etc. A measure of thickness of sheet metal or wire.

Girder. A flexural member which is the main or primary support for the structure, and which usually receives loads from floor beams and stringers.

Any large beam, especially if built up.

Girder Bridge. A bridge whose superstructure consists of two or more girders supporting a separate floor system of slab and floor beams, or slab, stringer, and floor beam, as differentiated from a multi-beam bridge or a slab bridge.

Any bridge utilizing large, built-up steel beams, prestressed concrete beams, or concrete box girders.

With reference to the vertical location of the floor system, plate girder spans are divided into two types, viz.:

1. Through bridges having the floor system near the elevation of the bottom flanges, whereby traffic passes between the top flanges.

2. Deck bridges having the floor system at or above the elevation of the top flanges whereby traffic passes above the girders.

Girder Span. A span in which the major longitudinal supporting members are girders. It may be simple, cantilever or continuous in type.

Gothic Arch. (*Pointed Arch.*) An arch in which the intrados surface is composed of two equal cylinder segments intersecting obtusely at the crown.

The Tudor Arch is a modification of the Gothic, produced by the introduction of shorter radius cylinder segments at the haunches thus rendering it a four-centered form or type.

Grade Crossing. A term applicable to an intersection of two or more highways, two railroads or one railroad and one highway at a common grade or elevation; now commonly accepted as meaning the last of these combinations.

Grade Intersection. The location where a horizontal and an inclined length of roadway or, instead, two inclined lengths meet in profile. To provide an easy transition from one to the other they are connected by a vertical curve and the resulting profile is a sag or a summit depending upon whether concaved or convexed upward.

Grade Separation. A term applied to the use of a bridge structure and its approaches to divide or separate the crossing movement of vehicular, pedestrian or other traffic, by confining portions thereof to different elevations. See OVERPASS.

Gradient. The rate of inclination of the roadway and/or sidewalk surface(s) from horizontal applying to a bridge and its approaches. It is commonly expressed as a percentage relation of horizontal to vertical dimensions.

Gravity Wall. See RETAINING WALL.

Grillage. A platform-like construction or assemblage used to insure distribution of loads upon unconsolidated soil material. See FOUNDATION GRILLAGE.

A frame composed of I-beams or other structural shapes rigidly connected and built into a masonry bridge seat, skewback or other substructure support to insure a satisfactory distribution of the loads transmitted by the superstructure shoes, pedestals, or other bearing members.

Grout. A mortar having a sufficient water content to render it a free-flowing mass, used for filling (grouting) the interstitial spaces between the stones or the stone fragments (spalls) used in the "backing" portion of stone masonry; for fixing anchor bolts and for filling cored spaces in castings, masonry, or other spaces where water may accumulate.

Guard Pier. (*Fender Pier.*) A pier-like structure built at right angles with the alignment of a bridge or at an angle therewith conforming to the flow of the stream current and having adequate length, width, and other provisions to protect the swing span in its open position from collision with passing vessels or other water-borne equipment and materials. It also serves to protect the supporting center pier of the swing span from injury and may or may not be equipped with a rest pier upon which the swing span in its open position may be latched. The type of construction varies with navigation and stream conditions from a simple pile and timber structure or a wooden crib-stone ballasted structure to a solid masonry one, or to a combination construction. In locations where ice floes or other water-borne materials may accumulate upon the upstream pier end, a cutwater or a starling is an essential detail. See FENDER PIER.

Guard Railing. (*Guard Rail, Guard Fence, Protection Railing.*) A fencelike barrier or protection built within the roadway shoulder area and intended to function as a combined guide or guard for the movement of vehicular and/or pedestrian traffic and to prevent or hinder the accidental passage of such traffic beyond the berm line of the roadway.

Guide. A member or element of a member functioning to hold in position and direct the movement of a moving part.

Guide Roller. A roller fixed in its location or position and serving both as a friction roller and as a pilot or guide for a part or member in contact with it.

Gusset. A plate serving to connect or unite the elements of a member or the members of a structure and to hold them in correct alignment and/or position at a joint. A plate may function both as a gusset and splice plate while under other conditions it may function as a gusset and stay plate. See SPLICE PLATE and STAY PLATE.

Gutter. See DRAIN.

Gutter Grating. A perforated or barred cover placed upon an inlet to a drain to prevent the entrance of debris gathered and brought to the inlet by the water stream.

Guy. A cable, chain, rod or rope member serving to check and control undulating, swaying or other movements, or to hold a fixed alignment or position a structure or part thereof by having one of its ends bolted, clamped, tied or otherwise fastened upon it, the other end being secured upon a part or member of the structure or upon a disconnected anchorage.

H

H-Beam. (*H-Pile.*) A rolled steel bearing pile having an H-shaped cross section.

Hand Hole. Holes provided in cover plates of built-up box sections to permit access to the interior for maintenance and construction purposes.

Hand Operated Span. A manpower-operated movable span to which the force for operating is applied upon a capstan, winch, windlass or wheel.

The terms "Hand Draw Bridge," "Hand Swing Bridge" and "Lever Swing Bridge" are applied to swing spans of hand-operated type.

Hand Rail. See RAILING.

Hanger. A tension element or member serving to suspend or support a member attached thereto. A tension member, whether a rod, eyebar, or built-up member supporting a portion of the floor system of a truss, arch or suspension span. In suspension bridge construction wire cable is used and the complete member is commonly termed a "suspender."

Haunch. A deepening of a beam or column, the depth usually being greatest at the support and vanishing towards or at the center. The curve of the lower flange or surface may be circular, elliptic, parabolic, straight or stepped.

Head. A measure of water pressure expressed in terms of an equivalent weight or pressure exerted by a column of water. The height of the equivalent column of water is the head.

Headwater. The depth of water at the inlet end of a pipe, culvert, or bridge waterway.

Headway. See CLEAR HEADWAY.

Heat Treatment. Any of a number of various operations involving heating and cooling that are used to impart specific properties to metals. Examples are tempering, quenching, annealing, etc.

Heel of Span. The rotation end of a bascule span.

Heel Stay. See SHEAR LOCK.

Hemispherical Bearing. A bearing which utilizes the ball and socket principle by having male and female spherical segments forming the bearing areas or surfaces of the interlocking elements, thus providing for movements by revolution in any direction.

In order to insure accurate adjustment of the mating elements it is essential that a pintle or other self-centering device be provided as a part of the construction details.

Hinged Joint. A joint constructed with a pin, cylinder segment, spherical segment or other device permitting movement by rotation.

Hip Joint. (*The Hip of Truss.*) The juncture of the inclined end post with the end top chord member of a truss. In the truss of a swing span, the juncture of the inclined end post located adjacent to the center of span, with the combined top chord and the connecting tie member between the swing span arms, is designated an "interior hip joint" or an "interior hip of truss."

Hip Vertical. The vertically placed tension member engaging the hip joint of a truss and supporting the first panel floor beam in a through truss span, or instead, only the bottom chord in a deck truss span.

Hook Bolt. 1. A bolt having a forged hook at one end used for essentially the same purposes as described for an eyebolt. See EYEBOLT. 2. A bolt having its head end bent at or nearly at a right angle with its body portion and, when in use, acting as a clamp.

Howe Truss. A truss of the parallel chord type originally adapted to wooden bridge construction but with the later development of metal bridge trusses it was adopted only to a limited extent due to the uneconomical use of metal in its compression members. The web system is composed of vertical(tension) rods at the panel points with an X pattern of diagonals.

Hydrolysis. A chemical process of decomposition in the presence of elements of water.

Hydroplaning. Loss of contact between a tire and the deck surface when the tire planes or glides on a film of water covering the deck.

I

Ice Guard. See FENDER.

Impact. As applied to bridge design—a dynamic increment of stress equivalent in magnitude to the difference between the stresses produced by a static load when quiescent and by a load moving in a straight line.

Impact Load. (*Impact Allowance.*) A load allowance or increment intended to provide for the dynamic effect of a load applied in a manner other than statically.

Indeterminate Stress. A stress induced by the incorporation of a redundant member in a truss or of an additional reaction in a beam rendering stress distributions indeterminate by the principles of statics.

In redundant beams or trusses the distribution of the stresses depends upon the relative stiffnesses or areas of the members.

Inelastic Compression. See COMPRESSION (INELASTIC).

Inspection Ladders. (*Inspection Platforms and Walks.*) Special devices or appliances designed to afford a safe and efficient means for making inspections and tests to determine the physical condition of a structure and to facilitate repair operations incident to its maintenance which must include these service conveniences. To prevent displacement they will be, in general, rigidly fixed upon the structure. However, certain types of structures are adapted to the use of movable platform devices for suspension from the railings or other parts which are or may be adapted thereto.

The term "catwalk" is applied to narrow permanent walks supported, usually, by brackets or by hangers and located below and/or above the bridge floor. This term is also applied to temporary walks used in the construction of suspension and other types of bridges as utilities facilitating the movements of labor and materials, and the supervision and inspection operations.

Intercepting Ditch. A ditch constructed to prevent surface water from flowing in contact with the toe of an embankment or causeway or down the slope of a cut.

Intergranular Pressure. Pressure between soil grains.

Intermittent Weld. A noncontinuous weld commonly composed of a series of short welds with intervening spaces arranged with fixed spacing and length.

Intrados. (*Soffit.*) The curved surface of an arch nearest its longitudinal (constructional) axis or axes. Properly speaking the intrados is the curve defining the interior surface of the arch.

J

Jack Stringer. The outermost stringer supporting the bridge floor in a panel or bay. It is commonly of less strength than a main stringer.

Joint. In Stone Masonry. The space between individual stones.

In Concrete Construction. The divisions or terminations of continuity produced at predetermined locations or by the completion of a period of construction operations. These may or may not be open.

In a Truss or Frame Structure. (1) A point at which members of a truss or frame are joined, (2) the composite assemblage of pieces or members around or about the point of intersection of their lines of action in a truss or frame.

K

Keystone. A stone of the crown string course of an arch. However, this term is most commonly applied to the symmetrically shaped wedge-like stone located in a head ring course at the crown of the arch, which thus exposed to view produces desired architectural effects. This head ring stone commonly extends short distances above and below the extradosal and intradosal limits of the voussoirs of adjoining string courses. The final stone placed, thereby closing the arch.

King-Post. (*King Rod.*) The post member in a "King-post" type truss or in a "King-post" portion of any other type of truss.

King-Post Truss. A truss adapted to either wooden or metal bridge construction. It is composed of two triangular panels with a common vertical. A beam or chord extends the full truss length.

In the through form of this truss the inclined members are struts and the vertical or King-post is a hanger. In the deck truss, the two inclined members become tie (tension) members and the vertical becomes a post (compression) member.

The King-post truss is the simplest of trusses belonging to the triangular system. However, it is described with equal accuracy as a trussed girder.

K-Truss. A truss having a web system wherein the diagonal members intersect the vertical members at or near the mid-height. When thus arranged the assembly in each panel forms a letter "K"; hence the name "K-Truss."

Knee Brace. A member usually short in length, engaging at its ends two other members which are joined to form a right angle or a near-right angle. It thus serves to strengthen and render more rigid the connecting joint.

Knee Wall. A return of the abutment backwall at its ends to enclose the bridge seat on three of its sides. The returned ends may or may not serve to retain a portion of the bridge approach material, but do hide the bridge seat, beam ends, and bearings.

Knuckle. An appliance forming a part of the anchorage of a suspension bridge main suspension member permitting free longitudinal movement of the anchorage chain at locations where it changes its direction and providing for elastic deformations induced by temperature changes and the pull exerted by the suspension member.

L

Lacing. See LATTICE.

Ladle Analysis. (*Ladle Test, Check Analysis.*) As applied to the chemical determination of the constituents of steel or other ferrous metals, the terms "ladle analysis" and "ladle test" are synonymous and are used to designate the analysis of drillings or chips taken from the small ingot or ingots cast from a spoon sample taken from each melt during the pouring (teeming) operation.

The term "check analysis" is applied to the analysis of drillings taken from the finished material after being rolled, forged or otherwise worked. It is primarily intended as a check determination of the results secured from the ingots made at the furnace. Specifications may provide a tolerance or margin of variation between the ingot and the finished material analyses.

Lagging. See FORMS.

Laminated Timber. Timber planks glued together to form a larger member. Laminated timber is used for frames, arches, beams, and columns.

Lap Joint. A joint in which a splice is secured by fixing two elements or members in a position wherein they project upon or overlap each other.

Latch. (*Latch Block.*) The device or mechanism commonly provided at one or both ends of a swing span to hold the span in its correct alignment when in its closed position, and in readiness for the application of the end wedges or lifts.

Latch Lever. A hand-operated lever attached by a rod, cable or chain to the latching device of a movable span and used to engage and to release the latch.

Lateral Bracing. (*Lateral System.*) The bracing assemblage engaging the chords and inclined end posts of truss and the flanges of plate girder spans in the horizontal or inclined planes of these members to function in resisting the transverse forces resulting from wind, lateral vibration, and traffic movements tending to produce lateral movement and deformation. See BRACING.

Lattice. (*Latticing, Lacing.*) An assemblage of bars, channels, or angles singly or in combination bolted, riveted or welded in inclined position upon two or more elements of a member to secure them in correct position and assure their combined action. When the bars form a double system by being inclined in opposite directions the assemblage is termed "double lattice." When so arranged the bars are commonly connected at their intermediate length intersections.

Lattice Truss. In general, a truss having its web members inclined but more commonly the term is applied to a truss having two or more web systems composed entirely of diagonal members at any interval and crossing each other without reference to vertical members. Vertical members when used perform the functions of web stiffeners. They may be utilized for connecting vertically placed brace frames to the girders.

Leaf. The portion of a bascule bridge which forms the span or a portion of the span of the structure.

Ledge Course. In masonry or concrete construction, a course forming a projection beyond the plane of a superimposed course or courses. The projecting portion may be wash dressed to permit an unobstructed flow of rain water down the wall surface. A ledge course differs from a belt or string course in having a projection only upon its topmost bed. This construction is also known as a "Ledger Course."

Ledge Rock. See BED ROCK.

Lenticular Truss. (*Fish Belly Truss.*) A truss having polygonal top and bottom chords curved in opposite directions with their ends meeting at a common joint. The chords nearly coincide with parabolic arcs. In through spans the floor system is suspended from the joints of the bottom chord and the end posts are vertical.

Lifting Girder. A girder or girder-like member engaging the trusses or girders of a vertical lift span and to which the suspending cables are attached.

Lift Span. A superstructure span moved by revolution in a vertical plane or by lifting in a vertical direction to free a navigable waterway of the obstruction it presents to navigation. See MOVABLE BRIDGE.

Link and Roller. An adjustable device or assemblage consisting of a hinged strut-like link fitted with a roller at its bottom end, supported upon a shoe plate or pedestal and operated by a thrust strut serving to force it into a vertical position and to withdraw it therefrom. When installed at each outermost end of the girders or the trusses of a swing span their major function is to lift them to an extent that their camber or droop will be removed and the arms rendered free to act as simple spans. When the links are withdrawn to an inclined position fixed by the operating mechanism the span is free to be moved to an open position.

Lintel Bridge. A bridge having a single span or a series of spans composed of slabs of stone or reinforced concrete spanning the interval or intervals between its substructure elements.

Lintel Stone. A stone used to support a wall over an opening.

Live Load. A dynamic load such as traffic load that is supplied to a structure suddenly or that is accompanied by vibration, oscillation or other physical condition affecting its intensity.

Loading Girder. A term applied to the girder or girders of a center bearing type swing span, located above the pivot pier and functioning to concentrate the superimposed load upon the pivot.

Location. The longitudinal line assumed for construction purposes, which may or may not coincide with the center line of bridge; together with the gradients upon the bridge and its approaches established upon the construction plans and/or on the bridge site preparatory to construction operations.

Lock Device. A mechanism which locks the movable span of a bridge in its "closed" position and prevents movement to "open" position until released. The device on a swing span may also be used to lock the span in its "open" position at times when wind or other conditions render this prevention of movement desirable.

Locking Mechanism. A general term applied to the various devices used for holding in their closed or traffic service position a bascule, vertical lift or swing span of any type. This term applies not only to the locking or latching appliance but includes also the levers, shafts, gears or other parts incidental to their service operation.

Longitudinal Bracing. (*Longitudinal System.*) The bracing assemblage engaging the columns of trestle and viaduct bents and towers in perpendicular or slightly inclined planes located lengthwise with the bridge structure and functioning to resist the longitudinal forces resulting from traffic traction and momentum, wind or other forces tending to produce longitudinal movement and deformation. See BRACING.

M

Margin. See TOLERANCE.

Masonry. A general term applying to abutments, piers, retaining walls, arches and allied structures built of stone, brick or concrete and known correspondingly as stone, brick or concrete masonry.

Masonry Plate. A steel plate or a plate-shaped member whether cast, rolled or forged, built into or otherwise attached upon an abutment, pier, column, or other substructure part to support the rocker, shoe, or pedestal of a beam, girder or truss span and to distribute the load to the masonry beneath.

Mattress. A mat-like protective covering composed of brush and poles, commonly willow, compacted by wire or other lashings and ties and placed upon river and stream beds and banks; lake, tidal or other shores to prevent erosion and scour by water movement action.

Meander. The tortuous channel that characterizes the serpentine curvature of a slow flowing stream in a flood plain.

Member. An individual angle, beam, plate forging, casting or built piece, with or without connected parts for joints, intended utlimately to become an integral part of an assembled frame or structure.

Milled. In steel fabrication, a careful grinding of an edge or surface to assure good bearing or fit.

Mortar. An intimate mixture, in a plastic condition, of cement, or other cementitious material with fine aggregate and water, used to bed and bind together the quarried stones, bricks, or other solid materials composing the major portion of a masonry construction or to produce a plastic coating upon such constructions.

The indurated jointing material filling the interstices between and holding in place the quarried stones or other solid materials of masonry construction. Correspondingly, this term is applied to the cement coating used to produce a desired surface condition upon masonry constructions and is described as the "mortar finish," "mortar coat," "floated face or surface," "parapet," etc.

The component of concrete composed of cement, or other indurating material with sand and water when the concrete is a mobile mass and correspondingly this same component after it has attained a rigid condition through hardening of its cementing constituents.

Movable Bridge. A bridge of any type having one or more spans capable of being raised, turned, lifted, or slid from its normal vehicular and/or pedestrian service location to provide for the passage of navigation. The movements of the superstructure may be produced either manually or by engine power.

Bascule Bridge. A bridge having a superstructure designed to swing vertically about a fixed or a moving horizontal axis. The axis may be the center of a hinge pin or trunnion, or it may be only a line fixing the center of a circular rotation combined with translation, (rolling lift bridge).

Vertical Lift Bridge. A bridge having a superstructure designed to be lifted vertically by cables or chains attached to the ends of the movable span and operating over sheaves placed upon the tops of masts or towers or by other mechanical devices functioning to lift the span to "open" position and to lower it into its "closed" position with its ends seated upon bridge seat pedestals.

Pontoon Bridge. A bridge ordinarily composed of boats, scows or pontoons so connected to the deck or floor construction that they are retained in position and serve to support vehicular and pedestrian traffic. A pontoon bridge may be so constructed that a portion is removable and thus serve to facilitate navigation. Modern floating bridges may have pontoons built integrally with the deck.

Retractile Draw Bridge. (*Traverse Draw Bridge.*) A bridge having a superstructure designed to move horizontally either longitudinally or diagonally from "closed" to "open" position, the portion acting in cantilever being counterweighted by that supported upon rollers.

Rolling Lift Bridge. A bridge of the bascule type devised to roll backward and forward upon supporting girders when operated throughout an "open and closed" cycle.

Swing Bridge. A bridge having a superstructure designed to revolve in a horizontal plane upon a pivot from its "closed" position to an "open" one wherein its alignment is normal or nearly normal to the original alignment. For a structure having its substructure skewed the design commonly provides for revolution in one direction only and through an arc less than 90°. The superstructure is balanced upon a center and its ends acting as cantilevers when the end bearings are released may be either equal in length or unequal with the shorter one counterweighted to permit free revolution movement. A swing bridge with its end bearings released may be supported: (1) upon a single center bearing; (2) upon a circular rim or drum supported upon rollers and (3) upon a center bearing and rim in combination.

Movable Span. A general term applied to a superstructure span designed to be withdrawn, swung, lifted or otherwise moved longitudinally, horizontally or vertically to free a navigable waterway of the obstruction it presents to navigation.

Mud Sill. A single piece of timber or a unit composed of two or more timbers placed upon a soil foundation as a support for a single column, a framed trestle bent, or other similar member of a structure.

A load distribution piece aligned with and placed directly beneath the sill piece of a framed bent is termed a "Sub-sill" although it may serve also as a mud sill.

N

N-Truss. See PRATT TRUSS.

Natural Slope. See ANGLE OF REPOSE.

Neat Line. (*Neat Surface.*) The general alignment position or the general surface position of a face or other surface exlusive or regardless of the projections of individual stones, belts, belt courses, copings or other incidental or ancillary projections in a masonry structure.

Neutral Axis. The axis of a member in bending along which the strain is zero. On one side of the neutral axis the fibers are in tension, on the other side in compression.

Normal Roadway Cross Section. The roadway cross section with its crown in countradistinction to the superelevated cross sections used upon horizontal curves of different degrees of curvature and the transition lengths required for their development.

Nose. A projection acting as a cut water on the upstream end of a pier. See STARLING.

Notch Effect. Stress concentration caused by an abrupt discontinuity or change in section. Such concentrations may have a marked effect on fatigue strength of a member.

O

Operator's House. (*Operator's Cabin.*) The building containing the power plant and operating machinery and devices required for the operator's (bridge tender's) work in executing the complete cycle of opening and closing a movable bridge span.

Overpass. (*Underpass.*) The applications of these terms are definitely indicated by their constructions. For any given combination of highways, railways, and canals, the basic element is a separation of grades. The use of these terms is fixed by the relative elevations of the traffic ways involved; for the lower roadway, the structure is an underpass; for the upper roadway, an overpass.

P

Packing Ring. See SEPARATOR.

Paddleboard. Striped, paddle-shaped signs or boards placed on the roadside in front of a narrow bridge as a warning.

Panel. (*Sub-Panel.*) The portion of a truss span between adjacent points of intersection of web and chord members and, by common practice, applied to intersections upon the bottom chord. A truss panel divided into two equal or unequal parts by an intermediate web member, generally by a subdiagonal or a hanger, forms the panel division commonly termed "subpanels."

Panel Point. The point of intersection of primary web and chord members of a truss.

Parabolic Truss. (*Parabolic Arched Truss.*) A polygonal truss having its top chord and end post vertices coincident with the arc of a parabola; its bottom chord straight and its web system either triangular or quadrangular.

Parapet. A wall-like member composed of brick, stone or reinforced concrete construction upon the retaining wall portion of an approach cut, embankment or causeway or along the outermost edge of the roadway or the sidewalk portion of a bridge to serve as a protection to vehicular and/or pedestrian traffic. While the terms balustrade and parapet are used, in a measure, synonymously, the latter is commonly regarded as applying to barriers of the block type without openings within the body portion. See BALUSTRADE.

Parker Truss. See PRATT TRUSS.

Pedestal. A cast or built-up metal member or assemblage functioning primarily to transmit load from one member or part of a structure to another member or part. A secondary function may be to provide means for longitudinal, transverse or revolution movements.

A block-like construction of stone, concrete or brick masonry placed upon the bridge seat of an abutment or pier to provide a support for the ends of the beams.

Pedestrian Bridge. See FOOT BRIDGE.

Penetration. When Applied to Creosoted Lumber. The depth to which the surface wood is permeated by the creosote oil.

When Applied to Welding. The depth to which the surface metal of the structure part (Structure metal) is fused and coalesced with the fused weld metal to produce a weld joint. See WELD PENETRATION.

When Applied to Pile Driving. The depth a pile tip is driven into the ground.

Pier. A structure composed of stone, concrete, brick, steel or wood and built in shaft or block-like form to support the ends of the spans of a multi-span superstructure at an intermediate location between its abutments.

The following types of piers are adapted to bridge construction. The first three are functional distinctions, while the remaining types are based upon form or shape characteristics.

Anchor Pier. A pier functioning to resist an uplifting force, as for example: The end reaction of the anchor arm of a cantilever bridge. This pier functions as a normal pier structure when subjected to certain conditions of superstructure loading.

Pivot Pier. Center Pier. A term applied to the center bearing pier supporting a swing span while operating throughout an opening-closing cycle. This pier is commonly circular in shape but may be hexagonal, octagonal or even square in plan.

Rest Pier. A pier supporting the end of a movable bridge span when in its closed position.

Cylinder Pier. A type of pier produced by sinking a cylindrical steel shell to a desired depth and filling it with concrete. The foundation excavation may be made by open dredging within the shell and the sinking of the shell may proceed simultaneously with the dredging.

Dumbbell Pier. A pier consisting essentially of two cylindrical or rectangular shaped piers joined by a web constructed integrally with them.

Hammerhead Pier. (*Tee Pier.*) A pier with a cylindrical or rectangular shaft, and a relatively long, transverse cap.

Pedestal Pier. A structure composed of stone, concrete or brick built in block-like form—supporting a column of a bent or tower of a viaduct. Foundation conditions or other practical considerations may require that two or more column supports be placed upon a single base or footing section. To prevent accumulation of stream debris at periods of high water or under other conditions the upstream piers may be constructed with cut-waters and in addition the piers may be connected by an integrally built web between them. When composed only of a wide blocklike form, it is called a wall or solid pier.

Pile Pier or Bent. A pier composed of driven piles capped or decked with a timber grillage or with a reinforced concrete slab forming the bridge seat.

Rigid Frame Pier. Pier with two or more columns and a horizontal beam on top constructed to act like a frame.

Pier Cap. (*Pier Top.*) The topmost portion of a pier. On rigid frame piers, the term applies to the beam across the column tops. On hammerhead and tee piers, the cap is a continuous beam.

Pilaster. A column-like projection upon a face surface rarely intended to serve as a structural member but instead functioning as an architectural treatment to relieve the blankness of a plane surface.

Pile. A rod or shaft-like linear member of timber, steel, concrete, or composite materials driven into the earth to carry structure loads thru weak strata of soil to those strata capable of supporting such loads. Piles are also used where loss of earth support due to scour is expected.

Bearing Pile. One which receives its support in bearing through the tip (or lower end) of the pile.

Friction Pile. One which receives its support through friction resistance along the lateral surface of the pile.

Sheet Piles. Commonly used in the construction of bulkheads, cofferdams, and cribs to retain earth and prevent the inflow of water, liquid mud, and fine grained sand with water, are of three general types, viz.: (1) Timber composed of a single piece or of two or more pieces spiked or bolted together to produce a compound piece either with a lap or a tongued and grooved effect. (2) Reinforced concrete slabs constructed with or without lap or tongued and grooved effect. (3) Rolled steel shapes with full provision for rigid interlocking of the edges.

Pile Cap. Concrete footings for a pier or abutment supported on piles. Also applied to the concrete below the pile tops when footing reinforcing steel is placed completely above the piles.

Pile Cut-Off. The portion of a pile removed or to be removed from its driven butt end to secure the elevation specified or indicated.

Pile Shoe. A metal piece fixed upon the point or penetration end of a pile to protect it from injury in driving and to facilitate penetration in every dense earth material.

Pile Splice. One of the means of joining one pile upon the end of another to provide greater penetration length.

Piling. (*Sheet Piling.*) General terms applied to assemblages of piles in a construction. See PILE.

Pin. A cylindrical bar used as a means of connecting, holding in position, and transmitting the stresses of, the members forming a truss or a framed joint. To restrain the pin against longitudinal movement its ends are fitted with pin nuts, cotter bolts, or both. The nuts are commonly of the recessed type taking bearing at their edges upon the assemblage of members. To prevent the loosening of the nuts and the displacement of the pins by vibration, joint movements, and other service conditions, the pin ends may be burred or they may be fitted with cotters.

Pin-Connected Truss. A general term applied to a truss of any type having its chord and web members connected at the truss joints by pins.

Pinion. The small driving gear on the powertrain of a movable bridge.

Pinion Bracket. The frame supporting the turning pinion with its shaft and bearings upon the drum girder or the loading girder of a swing span.

Pin Joint. A joint in a truss or other frame in which the members are assembled upon a cylindrical pin.

Pin Packing. An arrangement of truss members on a pin at a pinned joint.

Pin Plate. A plate or shape riveted or otherwise rigidly attached upon the end of a member to secure a desired bearing upon a pin or pin-like bearing; to develop and distribute the stress of the joint and/or secure additional strength and rigidity in the member.

Pintle. A small steel pin or stud, engaging the rocker in an exansion bearing, thereby permitting rotation, transferring shear, and preventing translation.

Pitch. The longitudinal spacing between rivets, studs, bolts, holes, etc., which are arranged in a straight line.

Plate Girder. An I-shaped beam composed of a solid plate web with either flange plates or flange angles bolted, riveted or welded upon its edges. Additional cover plates may be attached to the flanges to provide greater flange area.

Plinth. See FOOTING.

Plinth Course. The course or courses of stone forming the base portion of an abutment, pier, parapet or retaining wall and having a projection or extension beyond the general surface of the main body of the structure. See also BASE and FOOTING.

Plug Weld. (*Slot Weld.*) A weld joining two elements of a member or two members so assembled that an area of contact will be secured and the weld produced by depositing weld metal within circular, square, slotted or other shaped holes cut through one or more of the elements or members. This weld serves to unite the elements of a member or to join the members intersecting at truss at other joints of a structure.

Pointed Arch. See GOTHIC ARCH.

Pointing. The operations incident to the compacting of the mortar in the outermost portion of a joint and the troweling or other treatment of its exposed surface to secure water tightness or desired architectural effect or both.

Polygonal Truss. A general term applied to a truss of any type having an irregular or "broken" alignment of straight top chord members which forms with the end posts and the bottom chord the perimeter of a polygon.

Pony Truss. A general term applied to a truss having insufficient height to permit the use of an effective top chord system of lateral bracing above the bridge floor.

Pop-Out. Conical fragment broken out of concrete surface. Normally about one inch in diameter. Shattered aggregate particles usually found at bottom of hole.

Portable Bridge. A bridge so designed and constructed that it may be readily erected for a temporary communication-transport service; disassembled and its members again reassembled and the entire structure rendered ready for further service.

Portal. The clear unobstructed space of a through bridge forming the entrance to the structure.

The entire portal member of the top chord bracing which fixes the uppermost limit of the vertical clearance. See BRACING. The portal of a skew bridge is described as a "skew portal."

Post. A term commonly applied to a relatively short member resisting compressive stresses, located vertical or nearly vertical to the bottom chord of a truss and common to two truss panels. Sometimes used synonymously for column. See COLUMN.

Posted. A limiting dimension, speed, or loading, e.g., posted load, posted clearance, posted speed, indicating larger dimensions and higher speeds and loads can not be safely taken by the bridge.

Pot Holes. Small worn or distintegrated areas of bridge floor or approach surface concaved by the wearing action of vehicle wheels.

Pratt Truss. (*N-Truss.*) A truss with parallel chords and a web system composed of vertical posts with diagonal ties inclined outward and upward from the bottom chord panel points toward the ends of the truss except the counters required in midlength panels. The Parker Truss is an adaptation of the Pratt Truss by making the top chord polygonal in shape.

Priming Coat. (*Base Coat.*) The first coat of paint applied to the metal or other material of a bridge. For metal structures this is quite commonly a fabricating shop application and is, therefore, termed the "shop coat."

Protection Fence. See GUARD RAILING.

Protection Railing. See GUARD RAILING.

Q

Queen-Post Truss. A parallel chord type of truss adapted to either timber or metal bridge construction, having three panels with one of the chords occupying only the length of the center panel. Unless center panel diagonals are provided, it is a trussed beam.

R

Rack. A bar with teeth on one of its sides, designed to mesh with the gears of a pinion or worm. The rack is usually attached to the moving portion of a movable bridge and receives the motive power from the pinion.

Radial Rod. (*Spider Rod.*) A radially located tie rod connecting the roller circle of a rim-bearing swing span with the center pivot or center bearing casting.

Radial Strut. A radially located brace member of the drum construction of a rim-bearing swing span.

Railing. (*Handrail.*) A wooden, brick, stone, concrete or metal fence-like construction built at the side of the roadway, or the sidewalk, upon the retaining wall portion of an approach cut, embankment, or causeway or at the outermost edge of the roadway or the sidewalk portion of a bridge to guard or guide the movement of both pedestrian and vehicular traffic and to prevent the accidental passage of traffic over the side of the structure.

The term "handrail" is commonly applied only to railing presenting a latticed, barred, balustered or other open web construction.

Rake. The slope, batter or inclination from a horizontal, vertical or other assumed plane, of the sides of an embankment or other inclined earth construction; the batter of a face or other surface of masonry; of the plane of a truss side of a tower or other portion of a bridge superstructure or of any member thereof.

Ramp. An inclined traffic-way leading from one elevation to another. The general term used to designate an inclined roadway and/or sidewalk approach to a bridge and commonly applied to a rather steep incline.

Random Stone. A general term applied to quarried stone block of any dimensions whether intended for ashlar or for random masonry construction.

Range of Stress. The algebraic difference between the minimum and maximum stresses in a member or in an element or part thereof either computed to be produced by a given condition of loading or produced by its actual service loading.

Rebar. A steel reinforcing bar.

Redundant Member. A member in a truss or frame which renders it a statistically indeterminate structure. The structure would be stable without the redundant member whose primary purpose is to reduce the stresses carried by the determinate structure.

Re-Entrant Corner. A corner with more than 180° of material and less than 180° of open space.

Reinforcing Bar. A steel bar, plain or with a deformed surface, which bonds to the concrete and supplies tensile strength to the concrete.

Retaining Wall. A structure designed to restrain and hold back a mass of earth.

Buttressed Wall. A retaining wall designed with projecting buttresses to provide strength and stability.

Counterforted Wall. A retaining wall designed with projecting counterforts to provide strength and stability.

Gravity Wall. A wall composed of brick, stone or concrete masonry designed to be stable against sliding and rotation (overturning) upon its foundation or upon any horizontal plane within its body by virtue of its shape and weight.

Reinforced Concrete Cantilever Wall. A wall consisting of a base section integral with stem constructed approximately at a right angle thereto giving its cross section a letter "L" or an inverted "T" shape. The stem portion resists the horizontal or other forces tending to produce overturning by acting as a cantilever beam.

Rigid Frame Bridge. A bridge with rigid or moment resistant connections between deck slabs or beams and the substructure walls or columns, producing an integral, elastic structure. The structure may be steel or concrete.

In general this type of bridge may be regarded as a form of arch or curved beam having its intermediate intradosal section or portion either straight or slightly curved and its end sections located normal to the straight portion or to the tangent of the curved one at its center length position.

Rim Girder. See DRUM GIRDER.

Rim Plate. Toothed or plain segmental rim on a rolling lift bridge.

Ringbolt. See EYEBOLT.

Ring Stone. See VOUSSOIR.

Riprap. Brickbats, stones, blocks of concrete or other protective covering material of like nature deposited upon river and stream beds and banks, lake, tidal or other shores to prevent erosion and scour by water flow, wave or other movement.

Rise of an Arch. For a symmetrical arch; the vertical distance from the chord through its springing lines to the intrados at its crown.

For an unsymmetrical arch, assumed to be in a normal vertical position, the vertical distances from its springing lines to the intrados at its crown.

Riveted Joint. (*Bolted Joint.*) A joint in which the assembled elements and members are united by rivets. The design of a riveted joint contemplates a proper distribution of its rivets to develop its various parts with relation to the stresses and the purposes which each must serve.

A bolted joint differs from a riveted one only in the use of bolts as the uniting medium instead of rivets. The conditions of design are generally the same, but different allowable unit stresses are employed.

Roadway. (*Travel Way.*) 1. The portion of the deck surface of a bridge intended for the use of vehicular or vehicular and pedestrian traffic. 2. The top surface portion of an approach embankment, causeway or cut intended for the general use of vehicular or vehicular and pedestrian traffic. In general, its width corresponds (1) to the distance curb to curb; (2) to the distance between the outside limits of sidewalks; or (3) to the width of the roadway pavement or traveled way when no curbs exist.

Roadway Shoulder Area. (*Shoulder Area.*) The portion or area of the top surface of an approach embankment, causeway, or cut immediately adjoining the roadway, used to accommodate stopped vehicles in emergencies and to laterally support base and surface courses.

Rocker Bearing. A cylindrical, sector-shaped member attached by a pin or trunnion at its axis location to the expansion end of a girder or truss and having line bearing contact upon its perimetral surface with the masonry plate or pedestal, thus providing for the longitudinal movements resulting from temperature changes and superimposed loads by a wheel-like translation.

The design condition that the entire reaction stress is concentrated upon a line contact renders it especially essential that the masonry plate or pedestal be accurately leveled and that the rocker be carefully adjusted to secure a uniform even bearing thereon. A relatively large percentage of this type of bearings lack correct adjustment.

Rocker Bent. A bent composed of metal, reinforced concrete or timber, hinged or otherwise articulated at one or both ends to provide the longitudinal movements resulting from temperature changes and the superimposed loads of the span or spans supported thereon.

Rocker and Camshaft. An adjustable bearing device or assemblage consisting of a rocker bearing combined with a camshaft, properly mounted and geared to produce by its rotation a vertical lifting action, reacting upon a shoe plate or pedestal fixed upon the bridge seat. When installed at each outermost end of the girders, or the trusses of a swing span, the lifting action raises them to an extent that their camber or droop will be removed and the areas rendered free to act as simple spans. When the camshafts are revolved through an angle of 180° from their total or full lift position the rocker bearings are released and lifted and the span is free to be moved to "open" position.

Rolled Beams, Rolled Shapes. See STRUCTURAL SHAPES, WIDE FLANGE BEAMS.

Roller. 1. A steel cylinder forming an element of a roller nest or any other device or part intended to provide movements by rolling contact. The so-termed "segmental roller" consisting essentially of two circular segments integrally joined by a web-like portion is used in the construction of roller nests requiring relatively large bearing length with the least practicable shoe plate area and a correspondingly decreased weight of metal in the entire assemblage. 2. One of the wheel-like elements forming the roller circle of a rim-bearing swing span.

Roller Bearing. A single roller or a group of rollers so housed as to permit movement of a part or parts of a structure thereon.

Roller Nest. A group of steel cylinders forming a part of the movable end of a girder or truss and located between the masonry plate and shoe or pedestal to facilitate the longitudinal movements resulting from temperature changes and superimposed loads. Commonly the rollers are assembled in a frame or a box. Roller nests may be used for other services than those herein described. The term "Expansion Rollers" is sometimes used synonymously for roller nest.

Roller Track. The circular track upon which the drum rollers of a rim-bearing swing span travel. This is sometimes described as the lower track.

Roller Tread. See TREAD PLATES.

Rolling Lift Bridge. See MOVABLE BRIDGE.

Rubble. Irregularly shaped pieces of stone in the undressed condition obtained from the quarry and commonly ranging in size from relatively small usable pieces to one-man or two-man stones. This term is also applied to large boulders and fragments requiring mechanical equipment for handling. When shaped ready for use in rubble masonry, this stone is commonly described as "worked" or "dressed" rubble.

Run-Off. As applied to bridge design, the portion of the precipitation upon a drainage (catchment) area which is discharged quickly by its drainage stream or streams and which, therefore, becomes a factor in the design of the effective water discharge area of a bridge. Run-off is dependent upon soil porosity (varied by saturated or frozen condition), slope or soil surfaces, intensity of rainfall or of melting snow conditions, and other pertinent factors.

S

Saddle. A member located upon the topmost portion of the tower of a suspension bridge, designed to support the suspension cable or chain and to provide for its horizontal movements resulting from elastic deformations induced by temperature changes and the stresses incident to the service loadings.

Safe Load. The maximum loading determined by a consideration of its magnitudes and distributions of wheel, axle or other concentrations as productive of unit stresses in the various members and incidental details of a structure, permissible for service use, due consideration being given to the physical condition of the structure resulting from its previous service use.

Safety Curb. A narrow curb between 9 inches and 24 inches wide serving as a refuge or walkway for pedestrians crossing a bridge.

Sag. A deformation of an entire span; of any part of a span, or of one or more of its members from the horizontal, vertical, or inclined position intended as a condition of its original design and construction. This variation may result from elastic deformation of structural material; from irregularities produced by inadequate temporary supports during the progress of construction operations; or from incorrect adjustments and unworkmanlike procedures made a part of the work.

In existing structures sag may be attributable to (1) original construction irregularities; (2) to excessive stresses resulting from overloading; (3) to corrosion, decay or other deterioration of the structure materials, and (4) plastic flow of material.

The total deflection of the cable members of a suspension bridge. The so-termed "sag ratio" is the relation existing between the sag and the length of span.

Sag Rod. A rod usually fitted with threads and nuts at its ends; used to restrain a structure member from sagging due to its own weight or to external force or forces.

Sash Brace. (*Sash Stay, Sash Strut.*) A horizontal or nearly horizontal piece bolted or otherwise secured upon the side of a pile or framed bent between the cap and ground surface or the cap and sill, as the case may be, thus adding rigidity to the assemblage.

The horizontal member in a tier of bracing attached to a timber, reinforced concrete, or metal trestle bent or tower.

Scab. (*Scab Piece.*) A plank spiked or bolted over the joint between two members to hold them in correct adjustment and strengthen the joint.

A short piece of I-beam or other structural shape bolted, riveted or welded upon the flange and/or web of a metal pile to increase its resistance to penetration. Similarly, for the same purpose, a piece of dense hardwood fitted upon the flange and/or web and having bearing upon a lug angle at one or both its ends.

Scour. An erosion of a river, stream, tidal inlet, lake or other water bed area by a current, wash or other water in motion, producing a deepening of the overlying water, or a widening of the lateral dimension of the flow area.

Screw Jack and Pedestal. An adjustable device or assemblage consisting of a screw operated within a fixed nut and having upon its bottom end a pedestal-like bearing conjoined with it by a ball and socket or other equally adaptable articulation permitting its adjustment upon a shoe plate or pedestal fixed upon the bridge seat. When installed at each outermost end of the girders or the trusses of a swing span their major function is to lift them to an extent that their camber or droop will be removed and the arms rendered free to act as simple spans.

Scupper. (*Curb Inlet.*) An opening in the floor portion of a bridge, commonly located adjacent to the curb or wheel guard, to provide means for rain or other water accumulated upon the roadway surface to drain through it into the space beneath the structure. Bridges having reinforced concrete floors with concrete curbs may be effectively drained through scuppers located within the curb face surfaces.

Scupper Block. One of the short wooden pieces fixed between the wooden planks of a bridge floor and the bottom side of the wheel guard to provide open spaces beneath the latter for draining rain or other water accumulation from the floor surface.

Seam Weld. A weld joining the edges of two elements of a member or of two members placed in contact. This weld serves to form a continuous surface whether plane or curved, and to prevent infiltration of moisture between the parts. In general, it is not a stress carrying weld.

Seat Angle. (*Shelf Angle.*) A piece of angle attached upon the side of a column girder or other member to provide support for a connecting member either temporarily during its erection or permanently. The outstanding leg of the angle may be strengthened by a stiffener placed vertically beneath it.

Segmental Girder and Track Girder. These terms apply to the rolling lift type of bascule bridge combining circular rotation and translation movements in the "opening-closing" cycle.

The term "segmental girder" is used to designate one of the movable operating girders of a span or leaf to which a span girder or truss is rigidly attached. It commonly consists of a plate girder having its bottom flange curved to form a segment of a circle. This curved flange is fitted with tread castings which take line bearing contact upon the tread castings fitted upon the top flange of the supporting track girder with which they interlock to insure positive translation movement.

The term "track girder" is used to designate one of the plate girders or trusses intended to provide support for the movable span throughout an "opening-closing" cycle. Its tread castings fitted upon its top flange or chord form the track upon which the segmental girder moves by a rack and pinion-like action.

Segmental Rim. The curved rim or circular segment of a rolling lift bridge.

Seizing. The ligature of wire or other material applied upon a suspension bridge cable to hold the individual wires in satisfactory contact condition.

Separator. See SPREADER.

Shafts. Pieces conveying torsion stress only, which are, in general, used only in movable structures.

Shear Lock. (*Heel Stay, Tail-Lock.*) The device or mechanism provided at the heel of a bascule span to engage and hold the leaf in its closed position and prevent rotation.

Sheave. A wheel having a groove or grooves in its face surface. This term may be applied collectively to include both the sheave and its housing block.

Sheave Girder. A girder or girder-like member supporting the operating cable sheaves at the top of a tower of a vertical lift bridge.

Sheave Hood. A protecting covering placed above a sheave engaging the suspending cables of a vertical lift bridge to prevent accumulations of moisture, sleet and ice upon the sheave face.

Sheet Pile Cofferdam. In general a wall-like, watertight or nearly watertight barrier composed of driven timber or metal sheet piling constructed to surround the area to be occupied by an abutment, pier, retaining wall or other structure and permit unwatering of the enclosure so that the excavation for the preparation of a foundation and the abutment, pier or other construction may be produced in the open air. The alignment of the piles may be facilitated by the use of walers, struts and ties.

This type of dam is adapted to construction located in still or slow flowing shallow water. Its watertightness is sometimes rendered more complete by depositing earth material against the exterior side of the dam.

Sheet Piling. (*Sheeting.*) A general or collective term used to describe a number of sheet piles taken together to form a crib, cofferdam, bulkhead, etc.

Shelf Angle. See SEAT ANGLE.

Shim. A comparatively thin piece of wood, stone, or metal inserted between two elements, pieces or members to fix their relative position and/or to transmit bearing stress.

Shoe. In general, a pedestal-shaped member at the end of a plate girder or truss functioning to transmit and distribute its loads to a masonry bearing area or to any other supporting area or member. A shoe may be a cast or a built-up member; the base plate or plate-like part of which is commonly termed the "shoe plate," which may take bearing directly upon a masonry plate or upon an intervening expansion device.

Shore. A strut or prop placed in a horizontal, inclined or vertical position against or beneath a structure or a portion thereof to restrain movement.

Shoulder Area. See ROADWAY SHOULDER AREA.

Sidewalk. The portion of the bridge floor area serving pedestrian traffic only and, for safety and convenience to its users, commonly elevated above the portion occupied by vehicles.

Sidewalk Bracket. As applied to metal structures: A trianguar shaped frame attached to and projecting from the outside of a girder, truss or bent to serve as a support for the sidewalk stringers, floor and railing or parapet. In general, these brackets are in effect a cantilevered extension of the floor beams and are commonly connected to them by bars or other tension pieces designed to sustain the bending moment at the junction plane.

As applied to reinforced concrete structures: A cantilever beam commonly triangular in shape, attached to and projecting from the outside of a girder, truss, or bent to serve as a support for the sidewalk floor slab and the railing or parapet.

Sill. (*Sill Piece.*) The base piece or member of a viaduct or trestle bent serving to distribute the column loads directly upon the foundation or upon mud sills embedded in the foundation soil transversely to the alignment of the bent.

Silt. Very finely divided siliceous or other hard and durable rock material derived from its mother rock through attritive or other mechanical action rather than chemical decomposition. In general, its grain size shall be that which will pass a Standard No. 200 sieve.

Simple Span. A superstructure span having, at each end, a single unrestraining bearing or support and designed to be unaffected by stress transmission to or from an adjacent span or structure.

S-I-P Forms. See FORMS.

Skew Angle. As applied to oblique bridges; the skew angle, angle of skew or simply "skew" is the acute angle subtended by a line normal to the longitudinal axis of the structure and a line parallel to or coinciding with the alignment of its end.

Skewback. The course of stones, in an abutment or pier, located at the extremity of an arch and having its beds inclined (battered) as required to transmit the stresses of the arch. The bed adjoining the voussoirs forming the first string course of the arch ring will be normal to the axis of the arch. The individual stones of the skewback course are designated "skewback stones."

A casting or a combination of castings; or a built-up member designed to function as a skewback.

Skewback Shoe. (*Skewback Pedestal.*) The shoe or pedestal member, transmitting the thrust of a trussed arch or a plate girder arch to the skewback course or cushion course of an abutment or pier. Skewback shoes and pedestals are commonly hinged.

Slab. A thick plate, usually of reinforced concrete, which supports load by flexure. It is usually treated as a widened beam.

Slab Bridge. A bridge having a superstructure composed of a reinforced concrete slab constructed either as a single unit or as a series of narrow slabs placed parallel with the roadway alignment and spanning the space between the supporting abutments or other substructure parts. The former is commonly constructed in place but the latter may be precast.

Slag Inclusion. Small particles of slag trapped inside a weld during the fusion process.

Sleeve Nut. A device used to connect the elements of an adjustable rod or bar member. It consists of a forging having an elongated nut-shaped body with right- and left-hand threads within its end portions, thus permitting its adjustment with a wrench to provide a desired tension in the member.

Slenderness Ratio. Measure of stiffness of a member, expressed as the length of the member divided by its radius of gyration.

Slope. A term commonly applied to the inclined surface of an excavated cut or an embankment.

Slope Pavement. (*Slope Protection.*) A thin surfacing of stone, concrete or other material deposited upon the sloped surface of an approach cut, embankment or causeway to prevent its disintegration by rain, wind or other erosive action.

Slot Weld. See PLUG WELD.

Soffit. See INTRADOS.

Sole Plate. A plate bolted, riveted, or welded upon the bottom flange of a rolled beam, plate girder, or truss to take direct bearing upon a roller nest, bearing pedestal, or masonry plate. It distributes the reaction of the bearing to the beam, girder, or truss member. The sole plate may also function as a combined sole and masonry plate at the fixed end of a beam, girder, or truss.

Soldier Beam. A steel pile driven into the earth with its butt end projecting, used as a cantilever beam to support horizontal lagging retaining an excavated surface.

Spalls. Circular or oval depression in concrete caused by a separation of a portion of the surface concrete, revealing a fracture parallel with or slightly inclined to the surface. Usually part of the rim is perpendicular to the surface.

The pieces of spalled concrete themselves.

Span. This term has various applications depending upon its use whether in design, in field construction, or in its common nontechnical application, viz.:

When applied to design of a beam, girder, truss or arch structure. The distance center to center of the end bearings or the distance between the lines of action of the reactions whether induced by substructure or other supporting members.

When applied to the field construction of substructure abutments and piers. The unobstructed space or distance between the faces of the substructure elements. For arch structures this length is measured at the elevation of the springing lines. These lengths or dimensions are commonly referred to as "clear span length." See CLEAR SPAN.

The complete superstructure of a single span bridge or a corresponding integral part or unit of a multiple span structure. This application of "span" is rendered more specific when subdivided into: (a) Fixed Span: A superstructure anchored in its location upon the substructure and (b) Movable Span: A superstructure intended to be swung or lifted to provide an unobstructed waterway space for the passage of waterborne traffic.

Spandrel. The space bounded by the arch extrados, the substructure abutments and/or pier(s), and the roadway surface or other elevation limit fixed by the construction details.

Spandrel Column. A column superimposed upon the ring or a rib of an arch span and serving as a support for the deck construction of an open spandrel arch. See OPEN SPANDREL ARCH.

Spandrel Fill. The filling material placed within the spandrel space of a spandrel arch.

Spandrel Tie. A wall or a beam-like member connecting the spandrel walls of an arch and securing them against bulging and other deformation. In stone masonry arches the spandrel tie walls served to some extent as counterforts. In reinforced concrete spandrel arch spans spandrel tie walls may likewise serve as counterforts. See TIE WALLS.

Spandrel Wall. A wall built upon an arch to function as a retaining wall for the spandrel fill and the roadway in a spandrel filled structure; but, when the spandrel is not filled, to support the floor system and its loads. In wide structures having unfilled spandrels one or more interior walls may be used, thus providing a cellular construction when combined with tie walls. See TIE WALLS.

Specifications. A detailed enumeration of the chemical and physical properties determining the quality of construction materials together with requirements for handling, shipping and storage thereof; the conditions governing the loads, load applications and unit stress considerations of bridge foundation, substructure and superstructure design; the development of construction details and their applications incident to fabrication; erecton or other construction procedures pertinent to the production of serviceable bridge structures.

When general or so called "standard" specifications are used, it occasionally becomes necessary to supplement the requirements by items having specific application to a given bridge structure or group of structures. The special items may either designate and authorize departures from the "standard" or apply entirely to requirements and conditions not dealt with therein. The status of these supplemental or special specifications is commonly fixed by the "standard" specifications. Likewise the "standard" specification commonly recognizes the possibility of discrepancies between the specifications and the general plans and working (detail) drawings by fixing a coordination status for such occurrences.

Spider. The collar-like plate connecting the spider frame of a rim bearing or a combined rim and center bearing swing span to the pivot.

Spider Frame. The frame assemblage of struts, radial rods, spacer rings and roller adjusting devices holding the conical roller ring of a rim bearing or a combined rim and center bearing swing span in correct position with relation to the pivot.

Spider Rod. See RADIAL ROD.

Splay Saddle. A member at the anchorage ends of suspension bridge cables which permits the wires or strands to spread so that they may be connected to the anchorage.

Splice. This term has two applications depending upon its use whether in design or in shop and field construction, viz.:

When applied to design and the development of construction details: The joining or uniting of elements of a member, parts of a member or members of a structure to provide desired conditions for the transmittal of stress and the development of rigidity and general strength fulfilling the service requirements of the member or of the structure of which it is a part.

When applied to shop and field construction: the complete assemblage of parts used in producing the union of elements of a member or members of a structure.

Splice Joint. A joint in which the elements of a member or the members of a structure are joined by a splice plate or by a part or piece functioning to secure a required amount of strength and stability.

Spreader. 1. A cast or fabricated piece used to hold angles, beams, channels or fabricated pieces or parts in the locations or positions in which they function as parts of a member or structure. 2. A ring-like or sleeve-like piece placed upon a pin to hold the eyebars or other members assembled upon it in their correct member positions. This piece is sometimes described as a "pin-filler," or "packing ring."

Springing Line. The line within the face surface of an abutment or pier at which the intrados of an arch takes its beginning or origin.

Starling. An extension at the upstream end only, or at both the upstream and downstream ends of a pier built with surfaces battered thus forming a cutwater to divide and deflect the stream waters and floating debris and, correspondingly, when on the downstream end, functioning to reduce crosscurrents, swirl and eddy action which are productive of depositions of sand, silt and detritus downstream from the pier.

Statics. The branch of physical science which is concerned with bodies acted on by balanced forces. Therefore, these bodies are either at rest or static.

Stay-In-Place Forms. See FORMS.

Stay Plate. (*Tie Plate.*) A plate placed at or near the end of a latticed side or web of a compression or other member and also at intermediate locations where connections for members interrupt the continuity of the latticing. This plate serves to distribute the lattice bar stress to the elements of the member and adds stiffness and rigidity to joint assemblages.

Stem. The vertical wall portion of an abutment retaining wall, or solid pier. See also BREASTWALL.

Stiffener. An angle, tee, plate or other rolled section riveted, bolted or welded upon the web of a plate girder or other "built-up" member to transfer stress and to prevent buckling or other deformation.

A stiffener forged at its ends to fit upon the web and the web-legs of the flange angles of a plate girder is termed "crimped."

Stiffening Girder, Stiffening Truss. A girder or truss incorporated in a suspension bridge to function in conjunction with a suspension cable or chain by restraining the deformations of the latter and by distributing the concentrated or other irregularly distributed loads thus resisting and controlling the vertical oscillations of the floor system imparted to it by the cable or chain deformations.

Stirrup. In timber and metal bridges: A U-shaped rod, bar or angle piece providing a stirrup-like support for an element of a member or a member.

In reinforced concrete bridges: A U-shaped bar placed in beams, slabs or similar constructions to resist diagonal tension stresses.

Stirrup Bolt. A U-shaped rod or bar fitted at its ends with threads, nuts and washers and used to support streamer or other timber pieces of wooden truss structures suspended from the bottom chord.

Stone Facing. (*Stone Veneer, Brick Veneer.*) A stone or brick surface covering or sheath laid in imitation of stone or brick masonry but having a depth thickness equal to the width dimension of one stone or brick for stretchers and the length dimension for headers. The backing portion of a wall or the interior portion of a pier may be constructed of rough stones imbedded in mortar or concrete, cyclopean concrete, plain or reinforced concrete, brick bats imbedded in mortar, or even of mortar alone. The backing and interior material may be deposited as the laying of the facing material progresses to secure interlocking and bonding with it, or the covering material may be laid upon its preformed surface.

Strain. The distortion of a body produced by the application of one or more external forces and measured in units of length. In common usage, this is the proportional relation of the amount of distortion divided by the original length.

Stress. The resistance of a body to distortion when in a solid or plastic state and when acting in an unconfined condition. Stress is produced by the strain (distortion) and holds in equilibrium the external forces causing the distortion. It is measured in pounds or tons. Within the elastic limit the strain in a member of a structure is proportional to the stress in that member.

Allowable Unit Stress. As applied to the investigation of an existing structure in determining its adequacy for existing or prospective service; it is the stress per unit of area of the material of the entire structure or any portion or member thereof which is determined to be a safe unit for service use, due consideration being given to the quality of the material, physical condition, the adequacy of the construction details or other physical factors incident or pertinent to the service conditions to which they are or will be subjected and, if necessary, to the conditions contemplated to exist in the event of repair, replacement or strengthening operations.

Unit Stress. The stress per square inch (or other unit of surface or crosssectional area). The Allowable Unit Stress is: (a) Assumed in determining the composition and construction details of a memer or the members of a proposed structure, or (b) assumed for judging the safe load-capacity of an existing structure; while working stress is (c) produced in the members and parts of an existing structure when subjected to loads, impacts and other stress-producing elements and factors to which the structure is proposed to be or may have been subjected.

Working Stress. The unit stress in a member under service or design load.

Stress Sheet. A drawing showing a structure in skeletal form sufficient only to impart or suggest in conjunction with notations thereon its general makeup, major dimensions and the arrangement and composition of its integral parts. Special construction details may be shown by section views and sketches with or without dimensional data. Upon the skeletal outline of the structure or in tabulated form the drawing should show the computed stresses resulting from the application of a system of loads together with the design composition of the individual members resulting from the application of assumed unit stresses for the material or materials to be used in the structures. The assumed design load or loads should appear either in diagrammatic form with dimensions and magnitudes, or reference be made to readily available information relating thereto by a special note conspicuously displayed upon the drawing. A future investigation of a given structure to determine its reliability for a given load or combination of loads may be greatly facilitated and expedited by an adequate stress sheet record of its original design conditions.

Stringer. A longitudinal beam supporting the bridge deck, and in large bridges or truss bridges, framed into or upon the floor beams.

Structural Members. Basically these are of three types, viz.: (1) Ties: Pieces subject to axial tension only; (2) Columns or Struts: Pieces subject to axial compression only; (3) Beams: Pieces transversely loaded and subject to both shear and bending moment.

However, the arrangement of the members of a structure and the application of its design loads may embody combinations of these basic stress types.

Structural Shapes. As applied to bridge structures: The various types and forms of rolled iron and steel having flat, round, angle, channel, "I", "H", "Z" and other cross-sectional shapes adapted to the construction of the metal members incorporated in reinforced foundations, substructures and superstructures.

Structural Tee. A tee-shaped rolled member formed by cutting a wide flange longitudinally along the centerline of web.

Strut. A general term applying to a piece or member acting to resist compressive stress.

Sub-Panel. See PANEL.

Subpunched and Reamed Work. A term applied to structural steel shapes having rivet holes punched a specified dimension less in diameter than the nominal size of the rivets to be driven therein and subsequently reamed to a specified diameter greater than the rivet size.

This term is also applied to completely assembled and riveted members and structures in which the rivet holes have been produced by subpunching and reaming procedure.

Substructure. The abutments, piers, grillage or other constructions built to support the span or spans of a bridge superstructure whether consisting of beam, girder, truss, trestle or other type or types of construction.

Sump. A pit or tank-like depression or receptacle into which water is drained. The removal of the water so accumulated may be effected by pumping or by siphoning.

Superelevation. (*Curve Banking.*) The transverse inclination of the roadway surface within a horizontal curve and the relatively short tangent lengths adjacent thereto required for its full development. The purpose of superelevation is to provide a means of resisting or overcoming the centrifugal forces of vehicles in transit.

Superstructure. The entire portion of a bridge structure which primarily receives and supports highway, railway, canal, or other traffic loads and in its turn transfers the reactions resulting therefrom to the bridge substructure. The superstructure may consist of beam, girder, truss, trestle or other type or types of construction.

A superstructure may consist of a single span upon two supports or of a combination of two or more spans having the number and distribution of supports required by their types of construction, whether consisting of simple, continuous, cantilever, suspension, arch or trestle span-tower-bent construction.

Surcharge. An additional load placed atop existing earth or dead loads. In the case of abutments and retaining walls, the surcharge load is assumed to be replaced by an earth load of equivalent total weight.

Suspended Span. A superstructure span having one or both of its ends supported upon or from adjoining cantilever arms, brackets or towers, and designed to be unaffected by other stress transmission to or from an adjacent structure. The ordinary use of a suspended span is in connection with cantilever span construction.

Suspender. A wire cable, a metal rod or bar designed to engage a cable band or other device connecting it to the main suspension member of a suspension bridge at one end and a member of the bridge floor system at the other thus permitting it to assist in supporting the bridge floor system and its superimposed loads by transferring loads to the main suspension members of the structure.

A member serving to support another member in a horizontal or an inclined position against sagging, twisting or other deformation due to its own weight.

Suspension Bridge. A bridge in which the floor system and its incidental parts and appliances are supported in practically a horizontal position by being suspended upon cables which are supported at two or more locations upon towers and are anchored at their extreme ends. The cables constitute the main suspension members and commonly their anchorage may be one of three forms, viz.: (1) By extension of these members beyond the towers to the anchorages; (2) By fixing their ends upon the towers and backstaying the towers against overturning by the suspension members pulling upon them; (3) By an integral inclusion of the anchorages within the structure whereby the entire horizontal and vertical components of the main suspension member stresses are resisted by a rigid floor system construction functioning as a column, upon the extreme ends of which the main suspension members are securely connected. This form is commonly described as "self anchored."

Suspension Cable. (*Suspension Chain.*) One of the main members upon which the floor system of a suspension bridge is supported. Its ends may be fixed at the tops of towers which are backstayed to resist the horizontal components of the cable or chain stresses or instead it may rest upon saddles at the tops of two or more towers and be extended and fixed upon anchorage members. When the extension portions from the tops of towers to the anchorages do not directly support any part of the bridge floor, they function essentially as backstays; but when they engage floor suspenders located between the towers and anchorages they function as suspension cables for the end spans of the structure.

Sway Anchorage. (*Sway Cable.*) A guy, stay cable or chain attached at an intermediate length location upon the floor system of a suspension bridge and anchored upon the end portion of an abutment or pier or in the adjacent land surface to increase the resistance of the suspension span to lateral movement.

Sway Brace. 1. A piece bolted, or otherwise secured in an inclined position upon the side of a pile or frame bent between the cap and ground surface or the cap and sills, as the case may be, to add rigidity to the assemblage. See BRAC-

ING. 2. An inclined member in a tier of bracing forming a part of a timber, metal, or R/C bent or tower. 3. One of the inclined members of the sway bracing system of a metal girder or truss span. In plate girder construction the term X-brace is sometimes used.

Sway Frame. A complete panel or frame of sway bracing. See BRACING.

Swedge Bolt. See ANCHOR BOLT.

Swing Span. A superstructure span designed to be entirely supported upon a pier at its center, when its end supports have been withdrawn or released, and equipped to be revolved in a horizontal plane to free a navigable waterway of the obstruction it presents to navigation when in its normal traffic service position. See MOVABLE BRIDGE.

Swing Span Pivot. The center casting upon or about which the movable portion of a swing span revolves in making an opening-closing cycle.

In the center bearing type span, this casting functions not only as a pivotal member but also as the support for the movable span when the end lifting device is released.

In the rim-bearing type span this casting functions as a pivotal anchor member regulating the location of the movable parts throughout an opening-closing cycle but does not support the movable span.

In the combined center and rim-bearing type this casting functions as a support for a portion of the weight of the movable span when the end lifting device is released.

T

Tack Weld. A weld of the butt, fillet or seam type intended only to fix an element of a member or a member of a structure in correct adjustment and position preparatory to fully welding. Tack welds may be used to restrain welded parts against deformation and distortion resulting from expansion of the metal by atmospheric and welding temperatures.

Tail Lock. See SHEAR LOCK.

Tail Pit. See COUNTERWEIGHT WELL.

Tail Water. Water ponded below the outlet of a culvert, pipe, or bridge waterway, thereby reducing the amount of flow through the waterway. Tailwater is expressed in terms of its depth. See also HEADWATER.

Temporary Bridge. A structure built for emergency or interim use to replace a previously existing bridge demolished or rendered unserviceable by flood, fire, wind or other untoward occurrence, or instead, to supply bridge service required for a relatively short period.

Tendon. A prestressing cable or strand.

Tension. An axial force or stress caused by equal and opposite forces pulling at the ends of the members.

Throat. Of a fillet weld. The dimension normal to the sloping face of a fillet weld between the heel of the weld and the sloping faces.

Through Bridge. A bridge having its floor elevation more nearly at the elevation of the bottom than at the top portion of the superstructure, thus providing for the passage of traffic between the supporting parts.

Tide Gate. See FLOOD GATE.

Tie Plate. See STAY PLATE.

Tie Rod. (*Tie Bar.*) A rod-like or bar-like member in a truss or other frame functioning to transmit tensile stress.

Tie Walls. (*Spandrel Tie Wall.*) One of the walls built at intervals above the arch ring to tie together and reinforce the spandrel walls. See DIAPHRAGM WALL.

Any wall designed to serve as a restraining member to prevent bulging and distortion of two other walls connected thereby.

Toe of Slope. The location defined by the intersection of the sloped surface of an approach cut, embankment or causeway or other sloped area with the natural or an artifical ground surface existing at a lower elevation.

Toe Wall. (*Footwall.*) A relatively low retaining wall placed near the "toe-of-slope" location of an approach embankment or causeway to produce a fixed termination or to serve as a protection against erosion and scour or, perhaps, to prevent the accumulation of stream debris.

Toggle Joint. A mechanical arrangement wherein two members are hinged together, in fact or in effect, at a central location and hinged separately at their opposite ends; their alignment forming an obtuse angle so that a force applied at the common hinge location will produce a thrust acting at the end hinges, laterally to the alignment or direction of the original force.

Tolerance. (*Margin.*) A range or variation in physical or chemical properties specified or otherwise determined as permissible for the acceptance and use of construction materials.

Tower. 1. A three dimension substructure framework in a viaduct type structure having the vertical bents at its ends joined longitudinally by struts and braces thus rendering the assemblage so formed effective in resisting forces acting longitudinally upon the structure. 2. A four-sided frame supporting the ends of two spans or instead one complete span (tower span) and the ends of two adjacent spans of a viaduct; having its column members strutted and braced in tiers and the planes of either two or four sides battered. 3. A pier or a frame serving to support the cables or chains of a suspension type bridge at the end of a span. 4. A frame functioning as an end support, guide frame and counterweight support for a vertical lift span during an operating cycle.

Track Girder. See SEGMENTAL GIRDER.

Track Plate. The plate, toothed or plain, upon which the segmental girder of a rolling lift span rolls.

Track Segment. One of the assemblage pieces of the circular track supporting the balance wheels of a center bearing swing span or the drum bearing wheels of a drum or combined center and drum bearing span.

Transition Length. The tangent length within which the change from a normal to a superelevated roadway cross section is developed.

Transverse Bracing. (*Transverse System.*) The bracing assemblage engaging the columns of trestle and viaduct bents and towers in perpendicular or slightly inclined planes and in the horizontal or nearly horizontal planes of their sash braces to function in resisting the transverse forces resulting from wind, lateral vibration and traffic movements tending to produce lateral movement and deformation of the columns united thereby. See BRACING.

Transverse Girder. See CROSS GIRDER.

Travel Way. See ROADWAY.

Tread Plates. (*Roller Tread.*) The plates attached upon the bottom flange of the drum girder; shaped to form a circular surface taking a uniform even bearing upon the drum rollers and thereby transferring to them the live and dead loads of the superimposed structure. The assemblage of tread plates is sometimes described as the "Upper Track."

Tremie. A long trunk or pipe used to place concrete under water. A tremie usually has a hopper at its upper end.

The concrete placed under water by use of a tremie is often called tremie concrete. In placing tremie concrete, it is important that the mouth of the tremie be kept immersed within the mass of concrete already deposited to prevent the water from mixing with the concrete, thereby weakening or destroying it.

Trestle. A bridge structure consisting of beam, girder or truss spans supported upon bents. The bents may be of the piled or of the frame type, composed of timber, reinforced concrete or metal. When of framed timbers, metal or reinforced concrete they may involve two or more tiers in their construction. Trestle structures are designated as "wooden," "frame," or "framed," "metal," "concrete," "wooden pile," "concrete pile," etc., depending upon or corresponding to the material and characteristics of their principal members.

Trailing Wheel. See BALANCE WHEEL.

Triangular Truss. See WARREN TRUSS.

Trunnion. As applied to a bascule bridge. The assemblage consisting essentially of a pin fitted into a supporting bearing and forming a hinge or axle upon which the movable span swings during an opening-closing cycle.

Trunnion Girder. The girder supporting the trunnions on a bascule bridge.

Truss. A jointed structure having an open built web construction so arranged that the frame is divided into a series of triangular figures with its component straight members primarily stressed axially only. The triangle is the truss element and each type of truss used in bridge construction is an assemblage of triangles. The connecting pins are assumed to be frictionless.

Truss Bridge. A bridge having a truss for a superstructure: The ordinary single span rests upon two supports, one at each end, which may be abutments, piers, bents or towers, or combinations thereof. The superstructure span may be divided into three parts, viz.: (1) the trusses, (2) the floor system and (3) the bracing.

Truss Panel. See PANEL.

Trussed Beam. A beam reinforced by one or more rods upon its tension side attached at or near its ends and passing beneath a support at the midlength of the span producing in effect an inverted King post truss. The support, if a wooden block, is commonly termed a "saddle block" but, if a cast iron or structural steel member it is termed a "stanchion."

Tubular Truss. A truss whose chords and struts are composed of pipes or cylindrical tubes.

Tudor Arch. See GOTHIC ARCH.

Turnbuckle. A device used to connect the elements of adjustable rod and bar members. It consists of a forging having nut-like end portions right and left hand threaded and integrally connected by two bars upon its opposite sides thus providing an intervening open space through which a lever may be inserted to adjust the tension in the member.

Turning Pinion and Rack. The pinion to which the power to operate a swing span is applied and the circular rack fixed upon the pivot pier upon which the pinion travels to produce its rotation movement. When a swing span requires a very considerable amount of power to operate it, two operating pinions located at opposite sides of the circular rack or nearly so are commonly used to distribute the operating force upon the rack and its anchorage.

U

U–Bolt. A bar, either round or square, bent in the shape of the letter "U" and fitted with threads and nuts at its ends.

Underpass. See OVERPASS.

Uplift. A negative reaction or a force tending to lift a beam, truss, pile, or any other bridge element upwards.

V

Vertical-Lift Bridge. See MOVABLE BRIDGE.

Viaduct. A bridge structure consisting of beam, girder, truss, or arch span supported upon abutments with towers or alternate towers and bents or with a series of piers (cylindrical, dumbbell, rectangular or other types), or with any combination of these types of supporting parts.

In general, a viaduct is regarded as having greater height than a trestle. However, this notion is inconsistent with bridge engineering practice. A viaduct may be in all respects like a multiple span bridge.

Vierendeel Truss. A rigid frame consisting essentially of an assemblage of rectangles and trapezoids with no diagonal members. Its service in a bridge is the same as that assigned to a plate girder or a truss.

Voided Unit. A precast concrete deck unit containing cylindrical voids to reduce dead load.

Voussoir. (*Ring Stone.*) One of the truncated wedge shaped stones composing a ring course in a stone arch. The facing or head voussoirs are those placed at the terminations of a ring course.

W

Wale. (*Wale-Piece, Waler.*) A wooden or metal piece or an assemblage of pieces placed either inside or outside, or both inside and outside, the wall portion of a crib, cofferdam or similar structure, usually in a horizontal position to maintain its shape and increase its rigidity, stability, and strength. An assemblage of wale pieces is termed a "waling," or "strake o' wail."

Warren Truss. (*Triangular Truss.*) A parallel chord truss developed for use in metal bridge structures, wherein the web system is usually formed by a single triangulation of members at an angle to each other. There are no counters but web members near the center of a span may be subject to stress reversals and are to be designed accordingly. Verticals may or may not be used.

Washer. A small metal disc having a hole in its center to engage a bolt or a rivet. It may be used beneath the nut or the head of a bolt or as a separator between elements of a member or the members of a structure.

Water Table. The upper limit or elevation of ground water saturating a portion of a soil mass.

Waterway. The available width for the passage of stream, tidal or other water beneath a bridge, if unobstructed by natural formations or by artificial constructions beneath or closely adjacent to the structure. For a multiple span bridge the available width is the total of the unobstructed waterway lengths of the spans. See CLEAR SPAN.

Wearing Surface. (*Wearing Course.*) The surface portion of a roadway area which is in direct contact with the means of transport and is, therefore, primarily subject to the abrading, crushing or other disintegrating effect produced by hammering, rolling, sliding or other physical action tending to induce attrition thereof.

A topmost layer or course of material applied upon a roadway to receive the traffic service loads and to resist the abrading, crushing or other distintegrating action resulting therefrom.

Web. The portion of a beam, girder or truss, located between and connected to the flanges or the chords. It serves mainly to resist shear stresses. The stem of a dumbbell or solid wall type pier.

Web Members. The intermediate members of a truss extending, in general, from chord to chord but not including the end posts. Inclined web members are termed diagonals. A "tie" is a diagonal in tension while a brace or strut is a diagonal in compression. A vertical web member in compression is commonly designated a post, while one in tension due entirely to the external forces applied at its lower end, is designated a hanger. The joint formed by the intersection of an inclined end post with the top chord is commonly designated the hip joint or "the hip" end and the vertical tension member engaging the hip joint is commonly known as the hip vertical or the first panel hanger.

Web Plate. The plate forming the web element of a plate girder, built-up beam or column.

Wedge and Pedestals. An adjustable bearing device or assemblage consisting of a wedge operating between an upper and a lower bearing block or pedestal, and when installed at each outermost end of the girders or the trusses of a swing span, functioning to lift them to an extent that their camber or "droop" will be removed and the arms rendered free to act as simple spans. Furthermore, when installed beneath the loading girder of a center bearing swing span they serve to relieve the pivot bearing from all or nearly all live load and to stabilize the center portion of the span. When the wedges are withdrawn and the end latching device released, the span is free to be moved to an "open" position.

Lifting devices of the wedge and pedestal type may be used under the loading girder of a center bearing swing span in conjunction with rocker and eccentric, link and roller, or other end lifting devices at the ends of the span.

However, some swing spans of short length and placed in rather unimportant locations are designed to support both dead and live loads upon the center pivot and the ends of span are inadequately lifted with the result that they "end hammer" upon their pedestals.

Wedge Stroke. The theoretical travel distance a wedge must move upon its pedestal to lift the end of the arm of a swing span a distance equal to the vertical camber or "droop" of the arm due to elastic deformation minus the portion assumed to be provided in the field erection operation.

The actual elastic deformation of the arms of a given swing span may vary considerably from the theoretical due probably to temperature variations during the periods in which fabrication and erection are in progress, or to variation in the friction developed between the elements combined to form joints and to other incidental irregularities.

Weep Hole. (*Weep Pipe.*) An open hole or an embedded pipe in a masonry retaining wall, abutment, arch or other portion of a masonry structure to provide means of drainage for the embankment, causeway, spandrel backfill or retained soil wherein water may accumulate.

Weld. The process of uniting portions of one or more pieces, the elements of a member, or the members of a structure in an intimate and permanent position or status by (1) the application of pressure induced by the blow of a hammer or by a pressure machine, the portions to be united having been previously heated to a so-called welding temperature and the junction areas cleaned and purified by the application of fluxing material, or by (2) the use of a high temperature flame to preheat the metal adjacent to the weld location and when it has attained a molten temperature to add molten weld metal, in conjunction with fluxing material, in sufficient quantity to produce a fully filled joint when cooled or by (3) the use of the electric arc to obtain a molten temperature in the metal closely adjacent to the weld location and to supply in the arc stream molten filler metal and fluxing material requisite to produce by coalescence of the structure and electrode metals a fully filled joint.

The joint produced by the application of a welding process.

Weld Layer. A single thickness of weld metal composed of beads (runs) laid in contact to form a pad weld or a portion of a weld made up of superimposed beads.

Weld Metal. The fused filler metal which is added to the fused structure metal to produce by coalescence and interdiffusion a welded joint or a weld layer.

Weld Penetration. The depth beneath the original surface, to which the structure metal has been fused in the making of a fusion weld. See PENETRATION.

Weld Sequence. The order of succession required for making the welds of a built-up piece or the joints of a structure to avoid, so far as practicable, the residual stresses producing or tending to produce individual joint distortions and deformations of the structure or its members.

Welded Bridge. (*Welded Structure.*) A structure wherein the metal elements composing its members and the joints whereby these members are combined into the structure frame, are united by welds.

Welded Joint. A joint in which the assembled elements and members are united through fusion of metal. The design of a welded joint contemplates a proper distribution of the welds to develop its various parts with relation to the stresses and the purpose which each must serve, due consideration being given to factors productive of secondary stresses through weld shrinkage, warping and other conditions attending weld fabrication.

Wheel Base. A term applied to the axle spacing or lengths of vehicles. When applied to automobiles and trucks having wheel concentrations at the ends of the front and rear axles it is the length center to center of axles or the longitudinal dimension center to center of front and rear wheels.

Wheel Concentration. (*Wheel Load.*) The load carried by and transmitted to the supporting structure by one wheel. This concentration may involve the wheel of a traffic vehicle, a movable bridge, or other motive equipment or device. See AXLE LOAD.

Wheel Guard. (*Filloe Guard.*) A timber piece placed longitudinally along the side limit of the roadway to guide the movements of vehicle wheels and safeguard the bridge trusses, railings and other constructions existing outside the roadway limit from collision with vehicles and their loads.

Whiteway Lighting. The lighting provided for nighttime illumination along a road or bridge, as distinguished from sign lighting or colored regulatory and warning lights.

Wide Flange. (*Carnegie Beam.*) A rolled member having an H-shaped cross section, differentiated from an I-beam in that the flanges are wider and the web thinner.

Wind Bracing. The bracing systems in girder and truss spans and in towers and bents which function to resist the stresses induced by wind forces.

Wing Wall. The retaining wall extension of an abutment intended to restrain and hold in place the side slope material of an approach causeway or embankment. When flared at an angle with the breast wall it serves also to deflect stream water and floating debris into the waterway of the bridge and thus protects the approach embankment against erosion. The general forms of wing walls are:

(1) Straight—in continuation of the breast wall of the abutment.

(2) U-type—placed parallel to the alignment of the approach roadway.

(3) Flared—forming an angle with the alignment of the abutment breast wall by receding therefrom.

(4) Curved—forming either a convex or concave arc flaring from the alignment of the abutment breast wall.

The footing of a full abutment height wing wall is usually a continuation of the base portion of the breast wall but may be stepped to a higher or lower elevation to obtain acceptable foundation conditions.

A stub type of straight wing wall is sometimes used in connection with a pier-like or bent-like abutment placed within the end of an embankment. This type, commonly known as "elephant ear" or as "butterfly wing" serves to retain the top portion of the embankment from about the elevation of the bridge seat upward to the roadway elevation. The top surface is battered to conform with the embankment side slope.

Working Stress. See STRESS.

www.ingramcontent.com/pod-product-compliance
Lightning Source LLC
Chambersburg PA
CBHW081822300426
44116CB00014B/2453